Truly the Signs of an Apostle

Frank I. Snyder

Cover Photo: Bryan Stiekes
Cover Design: Noelle Stiekes

Copyright © 2011 Frank I. Snyder
All rights reserved.
ISBN:1463606753
ISBN-13:978-1463606756

CONTENTS

Acknowledgments

Introduction 7

1	The Analysis of Apostles	9
2	The Classifications of Apostles	15
3	The Preeminence of the Twelve Apostles	23
4	The Pledge to the Twelve Apostles	29
5	The Fulfillment to the Twelve Apostles	37
6	The Stewardship of the Twelve Apostles	47
7	The Certification of the Twelve Apostles	57
8	The Termination of the Twelve Apostles	71
9	The Legacy of the Twelve Apostles	83
10	Life in the Post-Apostolic Age	99
	Appendix One: Two Exceptions to the Rule	111
	Appendix Two: The Many Uses of the Word "Baptize"	127
	Appendix Three: Does Water Baptism Save?	137
	Bibliography	153

Acknowledgements

The author would like to gratefully acknowledge those that have been an encouragement to finish this work. First and foremost is my Savior, the Lord Jesus Christ, who changed me from an unforgiven sinner to a forgiven one and continues to change me through His transforming grace. All glory to Him!

To my wife Cyndy who has consistently urged me to use the abilities that the Lord has given me. If there were ever a validation of the providential working of God, it is the fact that he has brought together two people who are so different but who fill the gaps in each other's lives so well.

To my five children and their spouses who have nagged me periodically, "When are you going to get that book done?" Thank you for pestering me about this. However, please leave me alone about everything else I need to get done.

To the deacons and church family who have graciously given me time off to write, knowing that their preacher could not do it while having to maintain a full ministry schedule. You have helped me and have been co-laborers in this work. Many of you have gently prodded me to "finish the job." I hope you will be pleased.

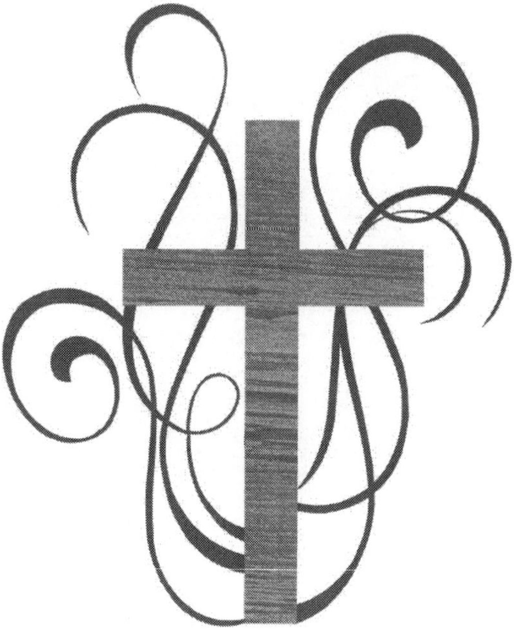

Introduction

This book is about the Apostles. Specifically, it's a book about the *Twelve* Apostles and their unique roll and calling by the Lord Jesus Christ. Connected with this study of the *Twelve* is an analysis of a phenomenon that is connected intimately with them – the endowment and empowering of the Holy Spirit. It is the author's contention that what is commonly referred to as the "baptism of the Spirit" was a unique and peculiarly *apostolic* event. I believe that the Bible is clear on this. Further, if this contention is true, then the claims and assertions of numerous popular preachers, so-called prophets, and self-identified apostles must be looked at with discerning scrutiny.

Many Pentecostal and Charismatic brethren will not be charmed by the contents of this book. Even among my Baptist brethren there are those that make claims concerning their personal possession of "Pentecostal power" through some dramatic post-salvation experience. I am sure that this book will not endear me to them either. God knows my heart and He knows, even if others do not, that this book was not written to take a poke at anyone.

The objective in writing this book is to give some clarity to a controversial subject within conservative Christianity and to be of help to folks that are confused. Make no mistake, my friend, confusion swirls like a tornado in evangelical/fundamental circles concerning the nature and work of the Holy Spirit. The solution to the confusion, in this writer's opinion, is a proper understanding of the relationship between the Lord Jesus Christ and His Twelve Apostles. Once that dynamic and vital relationship is understood, much of what is happening today in the name of the Holy Spirit is seen for what it really is -- "sounding brass, or a tinkling cymbal". (I Corinthians 13:1)

Though not a comprehensive work, considering the vastness of the related issues in the expansive charismatic movement, there has been a valiant and hopefully successful attempt at being readable, clear and faithful to the Scriptures.

(The reader should note that some of the Scripture verses contain bold text or notes in parentheses that were put in for emphasis or clarity by the author All Scripture used is from the King James Version.)

Chapter 1

The Analysis of the Apostles

*The importance of taking an honest look
at a serious subject:
Does It Take Getting Hit On the Head?*

Many years ago an acquaintance related how he and some others were in the backyard of a fellow charismatic believer.[1] Several folks had gathered there to worship. During the course of the activities a lady in the group experienced what is sometimes called being "slain in the Spirit" and fell backward. Unknown to her and to the other worshipers, there was a rock hidden in the grass. When she swooned under the "anointing" the woman tumbled backward, her head hitting the heretofore undisclosed rock. The result was a nasty gash requiring medical treatment. There was also a substantial amount of blood!

The impact of the incident, especially the blood, was not lost upon my acquaintance's young son who witnessed the event. "Daddy, why did God make that woman fall down and hit her head on a rock?" It was an innocent question of a little boy, but it was the first time his father had taken an objective look at what he was involved in.

---

[1] A charismatic is, generally, one who believes that the gifts and the empowering of the Holy Spirit are to be active today as they were in the Apostolic age. The defining characteristic of the charismatic movement is an emphasis upon the practice of ecstatic speech they would identify as the biblical gift of "tongues". There are some that would fall under the parameters of the charismatic movement that would reject many of the excesses associated with it and would dub themselves "non-cessasionists."

Was this of God? It was a legitimate question and one that ought to be asked frequently in these days of religious confusion. One would think that such reflective analysis would be the norm given the numbers of people who have claimed healing at the hands of those professing apostolic gifts and then subsequently dying of the illnesses and maladies of which they were "healed". One would think that the many instances of miraculous claims gone sour would cause at least one eyebrow to be raised (if not two). The fact that faith healers, who teach that healing is the inalienable right of believers through the atonement of Christ, get sick and die ought to cause at least a twitch.

Remarkably, events that would give pause and prompt questions from little boys seem to pass like water off a duck's back from people caught up in the emotion and the religious passion of the moment. The contents of this book will have little effect upon someone that refuses to "try the spirits whether they are of God..."(I John 4:1) and to rightly divide "the word of truth." (II Tim. 2:15)

If you are someone with at least one raised eyebrow who would rather not wait to be hit on the head before examining a very crucial biblical issue related to the working of the Spirit of God, then this book is for you. In this volume you will find some clarity to the mass confusion that exists in a religious world claiming mystical insights, supernatural power and even apostolic authority. There are many who are claiming the title of Apostle and assert that they are endowed with the same calling, ability and authority as the Apostles of old. They also maintain that miraculous occurrences typical of the apostolic age are supposed to be normal for today.

It is the thesis of this book that apostolic authority of the kind that existed in the New Testament church and which was characterized by powerful miraculous displays is long gone. It is the contention of this book that the existence and ministry of the Twelve Apostles and the miraculous demonstration of the power of the Holy Spirit were inseparably linked.

To some folks that acknowledgment may seem to be a sad or even a faithless assertion. On the contrary, it is a very good thing. If true (and it *is* true), then much of what is going on in the Christian religious world -- an abundance of which borders on the bizarre -- is at best "sounding brass, or a tinkling cymbal." (I Cor. 13:1)

In this book you will learn about the very special individuals given to the church by the Lord Jesus Christ. They were called *The Twelve*. You will also learn about the criteria for these special apostles -what facts *must* be true for anyone to claim that they were one of this elite group known as *The Twelve*. We will find out that these men received a special promise from Jesus that was given to them alone. That promise was fulfilled to them alone and gave them a special ability to impart a unique endowment of miraculous power that was typical of the early years of the church. This ability, that was the venue of the Twelve Apostles alone, has not been given to anyone else since!

What will knowing these things do for you, dear Reader? So glad that you asked! What the contents of this book will do for you is enable you to truly walk by faith, trusting in what is revealed in God's Word, the Bible. It is a fact that many who say they are living by faith are really living in doubt and looking for proof. They are seeking spiritual experiences and miraculous occurrences to give validation to their wavering faith and seem to be on an endless quest for the next spiritual "high."

Many believers are like surfers, endlessly looking to ride the perfect wave. That wave either never comes or they wipe out on the wave they thought was perfect. Then they start the process all over again. For many it is disappointing. It is frequently an emotional process that does not end well. All too often the end result is depression, defeat and disenchantment with the things of God.

Understanding the truths contained in this small volume will free confused believers from competing authorities in their lives. As a pastor of over 30 years I have found that many believers trust the Bible and....something else. They trust in the Bible *and* impressions, the Bible *and* experiences or the Bible *and* the pronouncements of the many self-appointed apostles and self-styled prophets who inhabit the religious world today. The result of these competing authorities has largely been chaos, confusion, heresy and disillusionment among believers. It has also increased skepticism among unbelievers.

It is the position of this writer that our New Testament faith was begun by the Savior Jesus Christ and conveyed by Him to those apostolic witnesses to the resurrected Christ appointed by Him for that purpose (I Cor. 15:1 - 11). It is the author's belief that we have an inspired record of that transmission in the Bible. As such, sincere believers should be satisfied with Christ and the Bible without seeking some esoteric or ecstatic experience being touted by some religious teacher or leader.

I would encourage you to approach the contents of this book as objectively as you can. That might be extremely difficult for those who tend to see biblical truth through an experiential or mystical grid. However, I would encourage you to ask the Lord to give you guidance and then plunge ahead. It is not difficult reading. It is not written for scholars and intellectuals. However, neither is it "bathtub" reading. I guarantee, though, that it will be a lot less painful than a crack on the head! I feel an anecdote coming on!

Matt Lincoln said that he was so consumed by the Spirit of God that he fell and hit his head while in church. As a result, Lincoln sued the Lakewind Church in Knoxville, Tennessee, for $2.5 million to compensate him for his medical bills. lost income, and the pain and suffering he endured from his injuries. Since his insurance company denied his claim for medical bills, Lincoln expected the church to pay his expenses. Lincoln had two surgeries since the June 2007 incident but said that he still felt pain in his back and his legs. The Lakewind Church's lawyers said that other congregants saw him on the floor laughing after his fall. They said he failed to look out for his own safety by making sure someone was there to catch him if he fell. [2]

"Daddy, why did God make that man fall down and hurt himself?" Hmmm!

---

[2] Courthouse News Service Knoxville TN ca: June 5, 2007

Chapter 2

The Classifications of Apostles

(capital "A" versus small "a" apostles)
"Be Verwy Quiet, We're Hunting Apostles!"
(An adaptation of the famous quote
from the consummate actor Elmer Fudd)

My six year old grandson was going to his first father/son retreat. He was excited at the prospect of this overnight adventure with his dad and looked forward to it with anticipation. At least he looked forward to it *until* he was told about the "snipe hunt." Snipe hunting has been a key feature of many a father/son outing. The problem is that no one seems to be able to explain exactly what a "snipe" is. Oh sure, the dictionary says it is a long- billed bird that inhabits marshes and is a species of crane. However, the snipes of father/son retreats are well established to be more sinister than that! The conversation between grandson, Dad and Grandpa went something like this:

"We are going on a snipe hunt!" says dad.

"What's a snipe?" the grandson asks.

"It's kind of an animal."

"What do they do?"

"They run around the woods and make funny noises."

"What kind of funny noises?"

(Grandpa and dad make funny noises and tell the kid to watch out if he hears any of those noises.)

"What do they do when they make noises?"

"They don't do anything, The noises are kind of like when a skunk puts his tail up right before he sprays that stinky stuff."

"Do snipes have rabies?"

"No, I have never heard of any snipe that has rabies. Just don't make him mad if you see one."

Now, the point of sharing this little anecdote is not to convey that the writer is a great big liar (along with his grandson's dad). The point is that sending a bunch of ignorant people out hunting for something that they have no clue about is ridiculous. It is especially ridiculous if the thing does not exist, but then, that's the fun of going snipe hunting. (Incidentally, the boy *was* set straight about snipes.)

We are going apostle hunting! Why are we doing this? Because there is, at times, some confusion among believers about apostles. There *are* different types of apostles spoken about in God's Word. Suffice to say at this point, that the word *apostle* is used in a general sense *and* in a specific sense. We might say there are apostles with a small case "a" and then there are Apostles with a capital "A".

Generic apostles
(apostles with a small "a")

The word "apostolos" in the Greek language, means "one that is sent on a mission" or, more generally "messenger". Recently, the United States Secretary of Defense was sent on a mission to help ease tensions between Pakistan and India. He was an "apostle" in that general sense. He was sent on a mission as a messenger from the United States.

Generally, the word "apostle" could apply to anyone sent on a mission. There were apostles in this general sense in the New Testament church. There were people called apostles who were not of those that we would typically think of as one of *the Twelve* Apostles. In this sense, the word "apostle" is used loosely.

Those who traveled with or associated with the Twelve Apostles were at times called apostles. Barnabas, though not one of the Twelve Apostles, was referred to as an apostle. The context and implication of Acts 14:4 is that Barnabas was looked upon as an apostle by association with the message of the apostles.

> "But the Jews stirred up the devout and honorable women, and the chief men of the city, and raised persecution against Paul and **Barnabas**, and expelled them out of their coasts." (Acts 13:50)

> "But the multitude of the city was divided: and part held with the Jews, and part with the **apostles**." (Acts 14:4)

Later at Lystra, the populace tried to offer a sacrifice to Paul and Barnabas and the Scripture records:

> "Which when the **apostles, Barnabas and Paul**, heard of, they rent their clothes, and ran in among the people, crying out..."(Acts 14:14)

Paul refers to Titus and several of his co-workers as messengers (apostoloi) to the churches.

> "Whether any do enquire of Titus, he is my partner and fellow helper concerning you: or our brethren be enquired of, they are the messengers (apostoloi) of the churches, and the glory of Christ. (II Cor. 8:23)

Paul refers to his first encounters with apostles shortly after his conversion and refers to James, the Lord's brother as an apostle:

> "But other of the apostles saw I none, save James the Lord's brother." (Galatians 1:19)

Neither Barnabas, Titus, or James were of the Twelve Apostles and yet all are referred to as such. So it is apparent that the term "apostle" was used in a general sense of special associates of those we know as the Twelve Apostles. They were messengers of and to the churches. However, it is also apparent that these were apostles in a *generic* sense and not part of or on a par with those referred to as the Twelve Apostles. They were *associates* of The Twelve. As such, they were distinct from those who were specially chosen and empowered by the Lord for unique ministry.

The Designated Dozen

The word "apostle" carries with it a special meaning when it is applied to those who became known as "The Twelve." Although at various times "The Twelve" had eleven or thirteen, they were still called "The Twelve". It was as if it were a team name such as the "Detroit Pistons" or the "Pittsburgh Steelers". These special apostles were known as "The Twelve." Whenever "The Twelve" were mentioned, everyone knew who was being talked about.

These Twelve Apostles were especially chosen by the Lord Jesus Christ from among those who followed Him.

> "And it came to pass in those days, that he went out into a mountain to pray, and continued all night in prayer to God. And when it was day, he called unto him his disciples: and of them he chose twelve, whom also he named apostles;..." (Luke 6:12-13)

> "And he ordained twelve, that they should be with him, and that he might send them forth to preach,... " (Mark 3:14)

These specially selected individuals became known as "The Twelve".

> " And he called unto him **the twelve**, and began to send them forth by two and two; and gave them power over unclean spirits;" (Mark 6:7)

> "And they were in the way going up to Jerusalem; and Jesus went before them: and

> they were amazed; and as they followed, they were afraid. And he took again **the twelve**, and began to tell them what things should happen unto him,…" (Mark 10:32)

> "And in the evening he cometh with **the twelve**...." (Mark 14:17)

> "Then said Jesus unto **the twelve**, Will ye also go away?" (John 6:67)

> " But Thomas, one of **the twelve,** called Didymus, was not with them when Jesus came." (John 20:24)

> "Then **the twelve** called the multitude of the disciples unto them, and said, It is not reason that we should leave the word of God, and serve tables." (Acts 6:2)

> "And that he was seen of Cephas, then of **the twelve**:…" (I Corinthians 15:5)

"The Twelve" was as much a designation as a number, meaning that these were people who were uniquely chosen to represent the Savior.

The Twelve Apostles were distinctive, select individuals that had a singular relationship with the Lord Jesus Christ.

Matthew's gospel tells us (Mt. 10:2-4) that the names of these twelve original apostles were:

Simon Peter
Andrew
James [the son] of Zebedee
John [the son] of Zebedee
Philip
Bartholomew
Thomas (also called Didymus)
Matthew
James the son of Alphaeus,
Thaddaeus (also called Lebbaeus)
Simon the Canaanite
Judas Iscariot

These were considered the Lord's main men.

Frank I. Snyder

Chapter 3

The Preeminence of the Twelve Apostles

These guys are really important!

The Twelve Perpetuated

This special group lost one of the original members whose name most of us are familiar with -- Judas Iscariot. That name has become almost synonymous with betrayal and disloyalty. Judas betrayed the Lord Jesus Christ and then afterward committed suicide (Mt.27:5).

That reduced The Twelve to eleven. Yet a replacement was chosen to maintain this designated group – "The Twelve". In Acts we see the selection process that replaced Judas and reaffirmed the special designation of these Twelve. Here a gathering of disciples took place to whom Peter spoke. Peter explained that Judas needed replaced.

> "And in those days Peter stood up in the midst of the disciples, and said, (the number of names together were about an hundred and twenty,) Men and brethren, this scripture must needs have been fulfilled, which the Holy Ghost by the mouth of David spake before concerning Judas, which was guide to them that took Jesus. For he was numbered with us, and had obtained part of this ministry. Now this man purchased a field with the reward of iniquity; and falling headlong, he burst asunder in the midst, and all his bowels gushed out. And it was

known unto all the dwellers at Jerusalem; insomuch as that field is called in their proper tongue, Aceldama, that is to say, The field of blood. For it is written in the book of Psalms, Let his habitation be desolate, and let no man dwell therein: and his bishoprick let another take."
(Acts 1:15-20)

He then explains that Judas' replacement needed to meet certain criteria. The disciple selected to be one of The Twelve needed to have been a personal witness of the earthly life, death, and resurrection of the Lord Jesus Christ. He should have been with the Lord Jesus during His earthly ministry along with the other eleven Apostles from the time Jesus was baptized by John the Baptist until His resurrection.

"Wherefore of these men which have companied with us all the time that the Lord Jesus went in and out among us, Beginning from the baptism of John, unto that same day that he was taken up from us, must one be ordained to be a witness with us of his resurrection." (Acts 1:21-22)

They asked the Lord for his wisdom in the choice between two -- Matthias and Barsabas.

"And they appointed two, Joseph called Barsabas, who was surnamed Justus, and Matthias. And they prayed, and said, Thou, Lord, which knowest the hearts of all men, show whether of these two Thou hast chosen, That he may take part of this ministry and apostleship, from which Judas by transgression fell, that he might go to his own place." (Acts 1:23-25)

Matthias was chosen to take his position as one of The Twelve.

> "And they gave forth their lots; and the lot fell upon Matthias; and he was numbered with the eleven apostles." (Acts 1:26)

So, it is pretty clear that The Twelve were distinctive from generic apostles and had a novel relationship with the Lord Jesus Christ. This was demonstrated in the initial selection by the Lord Jesus and affirmed later in the selection of a replacement for Judas.

The Twelve Elevated

These Twelve have a level of importance in the Scripture that is often underestimated. For example, it is evident that Jesus Christ endowed these men with special abilities. He also gave them special authority and promised that The Twelve are going to rule over the tribes of Israel.

> "And Jesus said unto them, Verily I say unto you, That ye which have followed me, in the regeneration when the Son of man shall sit in the throne of his glory, ye also shall sit upon twelve thrones, judging the twelve tribes of Israel." (Matthew 19:28)

> "That ye may eat and drink at my table in my kingdom, and sit on thrones judging the twelve tribes of Israel." (Luke 22:30)

Their imminent position is also seen in that the twelve foundations of the New Jerusalem have inscribed the names of the Twelve Apostles.

> "And the wall of the city had twelve foundations, and in them the names of the twelve apostles of the Lamb." (Revelation 21:14)

Regardless of one's interpretive approach to the book of Revelation, it is obvious that the Twelve Apostles had special significance to the Lord and were given special honor. These men were especially chosen by the Lord Jesus for a special role in the foundation of the church. (Ephesians 2:20) As such, they should be highly regarded.

However, a word of caution is in order at this point. Though these men should be *highly* respected, nowhere in Scripture do we see anyone *ever* praying to them, venerating them or directing petitions to them. We do not witness, either before or after they died, any sort of deference to them that might even remotely be considered worship. That kind of adoration is reserved for Deity alone. God is the only One Who is to be prayed to, petitioned, meditated upon or adored.

The believers in the early church, including the Twelve Apostles, were sinners saved by the grace of God, just like any other believer who places their faith and trust in

Christ today. The apostles, whether generic or special, had a profound sense of their own unworthiness. In fact, when folks tried to direct worship toward them, their reaction was intense against such behavior.

> "Which when the apostles, Barnabas and Paul, heard of, they rent their clothes, and ran in among the people, crying out, And saying, Sirs, why do ye these things? **We also are men of like passions with you**, and preach unto you that ye should turn from these vanities unto the living God, which made heaven, and earth, and the sea, and all things that are therein:" (Acts 14:14-15)

We find Paul saying...

> "This is a faithful saying, and worthy of all acceptation, that **Christ Jesus came into the world to save sinners; of whom I am chief**." (1 Timothy 1:15)

Peter writes, using personal pronouns, ...

> "For Christ also hath once suffered for sins, the just for the unjust, that he might bring **us** to God, being put to death in the flesh, but quickened by the Spirit:" (1Peter 3:18)

The Twelve Apostles and others were men, made of the same stuff as you and I. They are not to be petitioned, prayed to, bowed down to or given any kind of obeisance. However, we can and should admire them. They certainly deserve our respect as the caretakers of the early church and as those endowed with a special commission from the Savior! As we shall see in the next chapter, they were also the recipients of a special promise.

Chapter 4

The Pledge to the Twelve Apostles

Recipients of a Special Promise

It is important to remember in any discussion of the Twelve Apostles that they were a unique group as illustrated in the preceding chapters. They were a special group chosen by the Lord Jesus and were thought of as unique in the early church. They are going to have a special role in restored Israel and are an honored band of men. (This is so obvious in the Bible that it must be conceded.) The Twelve are a singular corps of disciples with a defined role, not only when the Lord chose them, but also in a special promise that He made to them.

Luke, the physician and earthly writer of the book of Acts, records to his friend Theophilus the account of this special promise in chapter one of that book. Note that Luke points out that the Lord Jesus gave instructions to his Apostles *"whom he had chosen"* referring to The Twelve. The following passage from Acts makes this clear.

> "The former treatise have I made, O Theophilus, of all that Jesus began both to do and teach, Until the day in which he was taken up, after that he through the Holy Ghost had given commandments unto **the apostles whom he had chosen**: **To whom** (the Twelve) also he showed himself alive after his passion by many infallible proofs, being seen of **them** (the Twelve) forty days, and speaking of the

things pertaining to the kingdom of God: And, being assembled together **with them**,(the Twelve) commanded **them** (the Twelve) that **they** (the Twelve) should not depart from Jerusalem, but wait for **the promise of the Father**, which, saith he, ye have heard of me. For John truly baptized with water; but **ye** (the Twelve) **shall be baptized with the Holy Ghost** not many days hence. When **they** (the Twelve) therefore were come together, they asked of him, saying, Lord, wilt thou at this time restore again the kingdom to Israel? And he said unto **them** (the Twelve), It is not for you to know the times or the seasons, which the Father hath put in his own power. **But ye** (the Twelve) **shall receive power, after that the Holy Ghost is come upon you** (the Twelve)**: and ye** (the Twelve) **shall be witnesses unto me** both in Jerusalem, and in all Judaea, and in Samaria, and unto the uttermost part of the earth." (Acts 1:1-8)

Luke asserts and records that Jesus met privately with His Apostles. He commanded them to stay in Jerusalem and wait for the promise of the Father. The promise referred to was the empowering presence of the Holy Spirit (Acts 2: 4-5,8.) This promise of the empowering presence of the Holy Spirit to The Twelve is repeated elsewhere in the Scripture.

> " And, behold, I send the promise of my Father upon you: but tarry ye in the city of Jerusalem, until ye be endued with power from on high." (Luke 24:49)

The Apostle John records this promise to the Twelve in his gospel.

> "If ye love me, keep my commandments. And I will pray the Father, and he shall give you another Comforter, that he may abide with you for ever; Even the Spirit of truth; whom the world cannot receive, because it seeth him not, neither knoweth him: but ye know him; for he dwelleth with you, and shall be in you. I will not leave you comfortless: I will come to you." (John 14: 15-18)

This promise of a Comforter, identified as the Holy Spirit, would come to them. This promise is repeated later on in the chapter.

> " These things have I spoken unto you, being yet present with you. But the Comforter, which is the Holy Ghost, whom the Father will send in my name, he shall teach you all things, and bring all things to your remembrance, whatsoever I have said unto you." (John 14:25-26)

The Purpose of the Promise

Why did the Lord Jesus make this promise to the Apostles? There were three basic reasons that the Lord tells His Twelve that He was sending the Holy Spirit. Again, we must look at the Gospel of John chapter fourteen.

Reason #1: The Holy Spirit Would Be Jesus' Comforting Presence

> " And I will pray the Father, and he shall give you another Comforter, that he may abide with you for ever; Even the Spirit of truth; whom the world cannot receive, because it seeth him not, neither knoweth him: but ye know him; for he dwelleth with you, and shall be in you. I will not leave you comfortless: I will come to you." (John 14: 15-18)

There are two Greek words commonly translated "another" in the New Testament. One means another of a *different* kind. The other means another of the *same* kind.

The Greek word for "another" in this passage (verse 16) is the word that means *another of the same kind,* meaning of the same kind as the Lord Jesus.

Bear in mind that Jesus has just told them that *He* was going away. But He would see to it that His Father would send another of the same kind as He to be with them. This Comforter is further identified as a Presence whose character is truth and Who would be "in" them in a way that, at the time of that writing, they were not currently experiencing.

Apparently, this powerful presence was at that time "with" them but not "in" them. The Lord Jesus may even have been referring to Himself as currently dwelling with them and would be in them in the Person of the Spirit! So the promised Holy Spirit, the Comforter, would be a replacement for Jesus after His departure. This idea is reinforced in Jesus' statement in verse 18 where he says, "I will not leave you comfortless: **I will come to you.**"

Reason #2: The Holy Spirit Would Be Jesus' Conduit of Truth

In addition to being a comforting presence to them, this Comforter, identified as the Holy Spirit, would instruct The Twelve and bring to their recollection everything that the Savior had said to them when He taught them during His earthly ministry. The fact that this promise is specifically to the Twelve Apostles is obvious in that *only those who had been taught by Jesus on this earth could be reminded of what they had previously been taught!* Those closest to Him during His earthly teaching ministry were these Twelve. Their limited memories were insufficient to recall all that the Lord had taught them. Therefore, the Lord promises a "Comforter" who will be with them in His stead and bring what He taught them to their remembrance. Note the following verses:

> "These things have I spoken unto you, being yet present with you. But the Comforter, which is the Holy Ghost, whom the Father will send in my name, he shall teach you all things, **and bring all things to your remembrance, whatsoever I have said unto you.**" (John 14: 25-26)

Later in John chapter 16, the Lord Jesus tells them that this Holy Spirit that they would later encounter would be a *continuing* conduit of truth from Him.

> "I have yet many things to say unto you, but ye cannot bear them now. Howbeit when he, the Spirit of truth, is come, he will guide you into all truth: for he shall not speak of himself; but whatsoever he shall hear, that shall he speak: and he will show you things to come. He shall glorify me: for he shall receive of mine, and shall show it unto you. All things that the Father hath are mine: therefore said I, that he shall take of mine, and shall show it unto you." (John 16: 12-15)

A primary purpose of this apostolic anointing by the Holy Spirit at Pentecost was to initiate a continuing ministry of interaction between the Savior and The Twelve through the Spirit. In addition to being a comforting presence to The Twelve, the Comforter would remind them what the Lord Jesus had already taught and would continue to teach through Him.

Reason #3: The Holy Spirit Would Enable an Empowered Witness to The World

The Lord Jesus Christ promised The Twelve that they would receive a special anointing of power from Him. The Father had promised that a special demonstration of the Holy Spirit's power would be manifested in their lives. Jesus pledged that He would implement this promise.

> "And, behold, I send the promise of my Father upon you: but tarry ye in the city of Jerusalem, until ye be endued with **power** from on high." (Luke 24:49)

In the context of the chapter, it is clear that the Savior is speaking primarily to His specially chosen Twelve. Two disciples were met by the Lord on a lonely road (Luke 24:33-ff). The resurrected Lord revealed Himself to them and they reported, in turn, to a gathering of the eleven Apostles (verse 33) and "those who were with them." We are not told who these others were. The primary relevance of the passage in this discussion is that the Apostles as the designated group were there. Thomas, apparently, was the only one missing on this particular occasion (John 20:24). The command is clear. The Lord Jesus instructs His Apostles to go to Jerusalem and wait there for the power that was going to be given them.

The promise is reiterated in Acts 1:5 "...For John truly baptized with water; but ye shall be baptized with the Holy Ghost not many days hence."

The promise the Lord made was a product of the Holy Spirit's special presence -- special power. In the Greek, the word translated "power" is "dunamis," the word from which we get our English word "dynamite". It is used again in Acts 1:8.

> "But ye shall receive **power**, after that the Holy Ghost is come upon you: and ye shall be witnesses unto me both in Jerusalem, and in all Judaea, and in Samaria, and unto the uttermost part of the earth."

So it is obvious that the Lord Jesus made a promise to the Apostles that they were to go to Jerusalem and wait there for the Holy Spirit to "come upon them". After this event, they would be empowered to be special witnesses unto the Lord Jesus Christ and His resurrection. This special endowment of power through, by and of the Holy Spirit is referred to in various ways in the Scripture. Sometimes it is referred to as the Holy Spirit "falling upon" someone as it is used in Acts 8:16.

> "(For as yet he was fallen upon none of them: only they were baptized in the name of the Lord Jesus.)"

Sometimes it is called the "baptism" or "immersion" into the Holy Spirit. [1]

> "Then remembered I the word of the Lord, how that he said, John indeed baptized with water; but ye shall be baptized with the Holy Ghost." (Acts 11:16)

The language and context used in the above passages make it clear that the Apostles were to go to Jerusalem where they would experience a unique empowerment by the Spirit of God.

Distinct from Regeneration

This promise made to The Twelve is *not* about the indwelling regeneration of the Holy Spirit that comes when anyone believes (being born again). Nor is this the filling of the Spirit that is supposed to be true of every believer resulting in spiritual fruit (Galatians 5:22-25). This was a promise made to the Apostles, in particular, to equip them for their upcoming ministry to the world. Was this promise ever kept to them? Absolutely!

---

1. For an in depth study of the use of the term "baptize" or "baptism", please see Appendix 2: The Many Uses of the Word "Baptize"

Chapter 5

The Fulfillment to The Twelve Apostles

Promise Made / Promise Kept

> "And when the day of Pentecost was fully come, they were all with one accord in one place. And suddenly there came a sound from heaven as of a rushing mighty wind, and it filled all the house where they were sitting. And there appeared unto them cloven tongues like as of fire, and it sat upon each of them. And they were all filled with the Holy Ghost, and began to speak with other tongues, as the Spirit gave them utterance." (Acts 2:1-4)

Many years ago, a co-worker in a factory told me that he had tape recorded a prayer meeting in his church. He asserted that when he played the recording later there was the sound of a rushing mighty wind on the recording of his church prayer meeting! This happened, he claimed, despite the fact that the participants heard no sound at the time the meeting was actually going on. He maintained that it was a replay of what happened at Pentecost in Acts chapter two. I asked him if there were slivers of fire in this meeting that rested on people, but he replied that there were not. *He* was convinced that a re-enactment of Pentecost had taken place in his church prayer meeting. *I* was convinced he needed to buy a new tape recorder!

The conclusion of this writer is that the events recorded in Acts chapter two concerning the special anointing of the Holy Spirit is a one-time event in history. In its details, it was never repeated in the New Testament and it has never been repeated in the almost 2000 years since it happened in Jerusalem. The event itself had two physical characteristics:

There was an audible sound of wind like a tornado or at least a strong gale force wind.

There was a visible manifestation of fire in the form of slivers of flame.

These peculiarities were never repeated in Scripture. They were a one-time manifestation indicating the unique nature of what was happening. It is also the fulfillment of the promise that the Lord Jesus made to The Twelve alluded to in Chapter three of this book. It is apparent that the events of Acts two are the culmination of the promise that the Savior made to The Twelve recorded in chapter one of Acts and elsewhere.

The Recipients of the Promise of Pentecost

A pertinent question that often arises in this discussion is whether believers other than The Twelve received this promised outpouring of the Holy Spirit's power at Pentecost? For example, Jerry Jensen has asserted that the promise of the Comforter, the Holy Spirit, was imparted to *everyone* present with the Apostles in the upper room and not just to The Twelve.

"Believers in various denominations, scattered throughout the world, are receiving the baptism of the Holy Spirit and are speaking with other tongues just as

the one hundred and twenty did on the day of Pentecost."[1]

It is sometimes maintained that the recipients of this special power included both men and women and that the power came upon all that were present in fulfillment of prophecy. Indeed, Peter did relate that what was then occurring was, in some sense, a fulfillment of the prophecy in Joel 2:28-29.

> "But this is that which was spoken by the prophet Joel; And it shall come to pass in the last days, saith God, I will pour out of my Spirit upon all flesh: and your sons and your daughters shall prophesy, and your young men shall see visions, and your old men shall dream dreams: And on my servants and on my handmaidens I will pour out in those days of my Spirit; and they shall prophesy:" (Acts 2: 16-18)

However, it is evident that Peter's citing of this prophecy in Joel was not an absolute fulfillment of the prophecy. There were aspects of Joel's prophecy that did *not* happen at Pentecost. Note the passage:

> "...And I will shew wonders in heaven above, and signs in the earth beneath; blood, and fire, and vapour of smoke: The sun shall be turned into darkness, and the moon into blood, before that great and notable day of the Lord come:" (Acts 2:19-20)

---

1. Jensen, Jerry, *Baptists and the Baptism of the Holy Spirit* Full Gospel Businessmen's Fellowship International 836 S. Figueroa St. Los Angeles 17, CA 1963 p.3

Honest evaluation of the events cited in verses 19-20 -- *wonders...blood...fire...smoke...darkened sun...blood red moon...* -- were not occurring in conjunction with the outpouring of the Spirit of God in Acts two. Peter's citation of this passage in Joel was used to assert that what was occurring before the eyes of the Jews at Jerusalem *paralleled* the prophecy in Joel, but did *not* literally *fulfill* that prophecy!

Plus, the reader will note in what follows that it was not all *sons and daughters* upon whom the Spirit was poured out at Pentecost, but only to The Twelve! The biblical evidence confirms this analysis and verifies that *only* the Twelve Apostles actually received this promise on that day.

As we have already seen, the Lord Jesus commanded the Twelve to go to Jerusalem to wait for the empowering presence of the Holy Spirit whom He would send. The Bible indicates that the **only** recipients of flaming tongues of fire indicating the fulfillment of the Spirit's coming was to The Twelve! What is the evidence of that? Read on!

Only The Twelve

In the first two chapters of the Book of Acts we find the following basic breakdown of chapter one:

Acts 1:1-11: Final instructions and the ascension of the Lord Jesus into heaven

Acts 1:12-14: The gathering of the 120 disciples, including the Twelve, in the upper room

Acts 1:15-29: The choosing of a replacement for Judas.

However, there is an apparent passing of time between the last verse of chapter one and the first verse of chapter two. The setting is no longer an upper room with 120 disciples. The subsequent verses in Acts chapter two reveal that the promised baptism of the Spirit came upon *The Twelve and not the 120 of Acts 1:12-14.*

This fact is revealed in the text of Scripture. In Acts chapter one and verse twenty-six, it states:

> "And they gave forth their lots; and the lot fell upon Matthias; and he was numbered with the eleven apostles." (Acts 1:26)

The text begins in chapter two, verse one, *still speaking of the now completed band of Apostles:*

> "And when the day of Pentecost was fully come, they (the Twelve including Matthias, referred to in Acts 1:26) were all with one accord in one place. And suddenly there came a sound from heaven as of a rushing mighty wind, and it filled all the house where they were sitting. And there appeared unto them cloven tongues like as of fire, and it sat upon each of them. And they were all filled with the Holy Ghost, and began to speak with other tongues, as the Spirit gave them utterance."
> (Acts 2:1-3)

Were the 120 people spoken of in Acts 1:15 included in this promised endowment of power or was this limited to the Twelve? Subsequent verses in the second chapter of Acts bear out that *only* The Twelve received this empowerment.

People from all over the world were in Jerusalem for the feast of the Passover and heard the Apostles speak in their own languages. Notice the stir that was created when those upon whom the tongues of fire had settled began to speak in other tongues (languages).

> "And there were dwelling at Jerusalem Jews,
> devout men, out of every nation under heaven.
> Now when this was noised abroad, the multitude
> came together, and were confounded, because that
> every man heard them speak in his own language.
> And they were all amazed and marveled, saying
> one to another, Behold, are not all these which speak
> Galilaeans? And how hear we every man in our
> own tongue, wherein we were born?" (Acts 2:5-8)

Some, when they heard the cacophony of languages being spoken, said that the Twelve were drunk and they were babbling nonsense.

> "Others mocking said, These men are full of new wine." (Acts 2:13)

Then Peter stood up with the eleven other Apostles and began to address the crowd of amazed and doubting onlookers who were questioning the sobriety of the apostles.

> "But Peter, standing up **with the eleven**, lifted up his voice, and said unto them, Ye men of Judaea, and all ye that dwell at Jerusalem, be this known unto you, and hearken to my words: For **these** (the eleven) are not drunken, as ye suppose ..."
> (Acts 2: 14-15a)

Peter then dispels their assertion that they were drunk and quotes an Old Testament prophecy about the manifestation of the Spirit. He then witnesses about the Lord Jesus Christ, after which the Jewish folks who were gathered there, reacted (verse 37). The crowd addressed its remarks to the Apostles who were with Peter.

> "Now when they heard this, they were pricked in their heart, **and said unto Peter and to the rest of the apostles,** Men and brethren, what shall we do?"
> (Acts 2: 37)

Those who believed then attached themselves to The Twelve and stayed with them.

> **"And they continued steadfastly in the apostles' doctrine and fellowship,** and in breaking of bread, and in prayers. And fear came upon every soul: **and many wonders and signs were done by the apostles."** (Acts 2: 42-43)

The implication is clear that The Twelve and not the 120 were the recipients of the special, empowering presence of the Holy Spirit at Pentecost!

Perhaps a review of the facts thus far is in order:

- Jesus told his special apostles to go to Jerusalem and wait there for His promised Comforter and empowerment. (See chapter 4)

- Peter stood up **with the eleven** (Acts 2:14) and refers to the men he is standing with as not being drunk as they, the Jews who heard them speak in other languages, were supposing (Act 2:15).

- The response of the Jews was directly **"to Peter and the rest of the Apostles**, Men and Brethren, what shall we do?" (verse 37)

- Verse 42 states that the crowd continued with the **Apostles'** doctrine and fellowship (which verse 37 indicates was Peter and the eleven).

- Verse 43 says that it was **the Apostles** who were the ones that did many wonders and signs.

The context and details indicate that initially, the only ones who had tongues of fire rest upon them and, in turn, spoke in tongues and performed other signs and wonders were the Twelve. It is clearly in the text of Scripture that this initial pouring out of the Holy Spirit's power at Pentecost was *not* to the 120 men and women gathered in the upper room in Acts chapter one. It was to the Twelve and to them alone in Acts chapter two. The significance of this will be seen later.

The Bible makes it clear that after this bestowment of power at Pentecost, special miraculous events were performed by twelve select men who were witnesses to the resurrection of Jesus Christ and were members of the band known as the Twelve Apostles. They were given a special manifestation of the Holy Spirit's power at Pentecost which the Lord Jesus promised they would receive in such passages as Luke 24:49 and Acts 1:8.

Again, what is evident is that the *initial* manifestation of the Holy Spirit's power, in fulfillment of our Lord's promise, was to the Twelve. Were there others in the New Testament who did miraculous deeds, spoke in tongues and such? Absolutely! The only point at this time is that the Apostles were the *initial* recipients who were given a special endowment of power of the Holy Spirit. This happened in completion of the promise made to them by the Lord Jesus Christ.

Promise Made! Promise Kept!

Frank I. Snyder

Chapter 6

The Stewardship of the Twelve Apostles

Custodians of a Special Gift

Picture if you will, a successful entrepreneur in the restaurant business who becomes the founder of a chain of restaurants with a common name. He began with a small business and built it up into a successful enterprise. His desire is to branch out into other communities and regions. In pursuit of that desire, he appoints a board of directors to establish franchises for his restaurant chain. A franchise is an exclusive right to bear the company name and market the food specific to the chain.

Each director has the authority to grant franchises to individuals they choose. Once someone is granted a franchise by a director, the owners of the franchise can operate a branch of the restaurant chain. The franchisee benefits from the owner's expertise, the quality of the food, and the name recognition of the chain. However, the franchise operator does not own the property or the business. Further, he does not have authority to grant franchises to others. That power was granted to the directors by the owner and is non-transferable. The franchise owners are doing business through the authority granted them by the board of directors. However, the franchise owners do not have the power to grant franchises to others. That authority is granted to the directors alone by the founder.

The scenario above is analogous to what occurred in the early church. The Twelve were the board of directors of the early church. The Lord Jesus Christ, in fulfillment of His promise to them, sent them a special empowerment of the Holy Spirit recorded in Acts two. This power manifested itself initially in them being able to speak in languages that they had never learned (Acts 2:5-12). In the same chapter we learn that other miraculous events began to be seen through these Apostles (Acts 2:43).

Later, we learn that there were others who were not apostles who began to do miraculous deeds in similar fashion to what The Twelve did in Acts two. However, there was no record of a rushing mighty wind or flames settling on *them.* How was it that others began to do these things? How did they receive this power to do signs and wonders or speak in tongues? The answer is that they were given this power by the Lord through the Twelve! What is the biblical basis for this? Read on!

In Acts chapter eight, Philip the evangelist, was sent by God to preach in Samaria. Philip was doing miraculous activities there. A sorcerer by the name of Simon became a professed convert and began to accompany Philip.

> "But there was a certain man, called Simon,
> which beforetime in the same city used sorcery, and
> bewitched the people of Samaria, giving out that
> himself was some great one: To whom they all
> gave heed, from the least to the greatest, saying, This
> man is the great power of God. And to him they
> had regard, because that of long time he had
> bewitched them with sorceries. But when they

believed Philip preaching the things concerning the kingdom of God, and the name of Jesus Christ, they were baptized, both men and women. Then Simon himself believed also: and when he was baptized, **he continued with Philip, and wondered, beholding the miracles and signs which were done.***"*
(Acts 8:9-13)

The narrative then relates that the Apostles heard about the conversion of the Samaritans under Philip's ministry and sent two of the Twelve Apostles, Peter and John to assist in the ministry to the Samaritans:

> "Now when the apostles which were at Jerusalem heard that Samaria had received the word of God, they sent unto them Peter and John: Who, when they were come down, prayed for them, that they might receive the Holy Ghost: (For as yet he was fallen upon none of them: only they were baptized in the name of the Lord Jesus.) **Then laid they** (the Apostles) **their hands on them** (the new converts), **and they** (the new converts) **received the Holy Ghost.**" (Acts 9:14-17)

Reader, please note that two members of the special group, The Twelve, *not* Philip, laid their hands upon the Samaritan believers and they received this empowering presence of the Holy Spirit. The villain in this story, Simon, noted that *the falling of the Holy Spirit came through the Apostles.* Simon then tried to strike a financial deal with Peter and John.

"And when **Simon saw that through laying on of the apostles' hands the Holy Ghost was given**, he offered them money, Saying, Give me also this power, that on whomsoever I lay hands, he may receive the Holy Ghost. But Peter said unto him, Thy money perish with thee, because thou hast thought that the gift of God may be purchased with money." (Acts 9:18-20)

It is important to note that Simon was *not* asking to buy the *presence* of the Holy Spirit or miraculous abilities through the Holy Spirit. He was seeking to buy the *ability to impart* the Holy Spirit!

Please note the sequence:

- Simon beheld the miracles and signs that Philip did (Acts 8:13)

- Simon noted that the miracles and sign power were bestowed by the Apostles' hands and not through Philip. He did not try to purchase it from Philip even though the text says that Philip did miracles in Simon's presence. (Acts 8:13)

- Simon tried to purchase the ability to impart the Holy Spirit after he observed that Peter and John possessed this ability. (Acts 8:18-19)

It is important to note that it is not the ability to do miracles that Simon wished to purchase. He had already observed Philip doing signs and wonders (see Acts 8:6-7,13). Simon wanted the ability to bestow this special endowment of the Holy Spirit, a power reserved for the Twelve Apostles, that *resulted* in the ability to do the miraculous.

Philip had the ability to do miraculous deeds, but he did *not* have the ability to give the special endowment of the Holy Spirit that resulted in the ability to do the miraculous deeds. It was apparent that only the Apostles could do that! Otherwise Simon would have approached Philip to purchase that power. However, Philip did not possess this power. Philip had the power to do miracles but not the power to impart the ability to do miracles.

When did Philip get this power to do miracles? It is hard to say with certainty. Philip possibly got it at the same time that others did in Acts chapter six. There is no record of miraculous events done by Philip until after there was a laying on of hands by the Apostles. Note that in Acts six, the Apostles laid hands and prayed for, among others, Stephan and Philip. These two subsequently evidenced supernatural power. Notice the pertinent details in the following passages concerning both Philip and Stephan.

Stephan is the first "non-Apostle" recorded doing miraculous deeds.

> "And the saying pleased the whole multitude: and they chose **Stephen**, a man full of faith and of the Holy Ghost, and **Philip**, and Prochorus, and Nicanor, and Timon, and Parmenas, and Nicolas a proselyte of Antioch: Whom they set before the apostles: and **when they had prayed, they laid their hands on**

them. And the word of God increased; and the number of the disciples multiplied in Jerusalem greatly; and a great company of the priests were obedient to the faith. **And Stephen, full of faith and power, did great wonders and miracles among the people.** " (Acts 6:5-8)

Philip, another of these seven deacons, entered active ministry as an evangelist and went and preached in Samaria accompanied by miraculous deeds.

"Then **Philip** went down to the city of Samaria, and preached Christ unto them. And the people with one accord gave heed unto those things which **Philip** spake, **hearing and seeing the miracles which he did.** For unclean spirits, crying with loud voice, came out of many that were possessed with them: and many taken with palsies, and that were lame, were healed. And there was great joy in that city." (Acts 8:5-7)

Admittedly, *when* Stephan and Philip received this power is up for debate. What is not debatable is that they did not impart this power. This ability was reserved for The Twelve. This power had been promised by the Lord Jesus Christ to The Twelve. It was bestowed upon The Twelve. *The special endowment to The Twelve at Pentecost made them able to do miraculous events themselves and enabled them to give this special endowment of power to others.* However, those to whom it was given could not, in turn, give it to others.

The Twelve were the Board of Directors of the early church. They were the means through which manifestations of the power of God were given to various individual believers. The recipients possessed a limited capacity of this power but did not possess the power to transfer it to others.

This unique ability of *transfer* was a part of what it meant to be an Apostle. In every case of the manifestation of miraculous events in the New Testament, it is *by or in the presence of* an Apostle and in conjunction with them praying for and/or touching others. After this contact with The Twelve, the recipients were enabled to do the miraculous deeds recorded in Scripture.

The Acts Four Outpouring

There is an account in Acts chapter four that is said to be another outpouring of the Holy Spirit which was much broader than upon just *The Twelve* at Pentecost. Sometimes it is argued that events recorded there indicate a broad outpouring of the Holy Spirit to a multitude of people. However, an analysis of the passage indicates that the Apostles were the primary individuals preaching Christ and through whom the witness of the Spirit was given by miraculous events. Below is the narrative.

> "But Peter and John answered and said unto them, Whether it be right in the sight of God to hearken unto you more than unto God, judge ye. For we cannot but speak the things which we have seen and heard. So when they had further threatened them, they let them go, finding nothing how they might punish them, because of the people: for all men

glorified God for that which was done. For the man was above forty years old, on whom this miracle of healing was showed.

"And being let go, they went to their own company, and reported all that the chief priests and elders had said unto them. And when they heard that, they lifted up their voice to God with one accord, and said, Lord, thou art God, which hast made heaven, and earth, and the sea, and all that in them is: Who by the mouth of thy servant David hast said, Why did the heathen rage, and the people imagine vain things? The kings of the earth stood up, and the rulers were gathered together against the Lord, and against his Christ. For of a truth against thy holy child Jesus, whom thou hast anointed, both Herod, and Pontius Pilate, with the Gentiles, and the people of Israel, were gathered together, For to do whatsoever thy hand and thy counsel determined before to be done. And now, Lord, behold their threatenings: and grant unto thy servants, that with all boldness they may speak thy word, By stretching forth thine hand to heal; and that signs and wonders may be done by the name of thy holy child Jesus. And when they had prayed, the place was shaken where they were assembled together; and they were all filled with the Holy Ghost, and they spake the word of God with boldness.

"And the multitude of them that believed were of one heart and of one soul: neither said any of them that ought of the things which he possessed was his own; but they had all things common. And with great power gave the apostles witness of the resurrection of the Lord Jesus: and great grace was upon them all. Neither was there any among them that lacked: for as many as were possessors of lands or houses sold them, and brought the prices of the things that were sold, And laid them down at the apostles' feet: and distribution was made unto every man according as he had need." (Acts 4:19-32)

Note the details of the chapter.

- -Peter and John had been detained by the Sanhedrin after an impotent man was healed. (Acts 3)

- -Upon their release they went to "their own company" (Acts 4:23), suggesting that they rejoined the other Apostles.

- -Peter and John related the events and the threats of the Jewish leadership and had a prayer meeting together. They prayed that they would be granted boldness and power in their witness. (Acts 4:29-31)

- -God shook the place where they were, filled them with the Holy Spirit and poured out blessing upon them resulting in a multitude believing on Christ (verse 32). The summation of the narrative is given in verse 33 and suggests that the ministry of preaching and the miraculous occurrence referred to the ministry of The Twelve Apostles.

> " And with great power gave the **apostles** witness of the resurrection of the Lord Jesus: and great grace was upon them all. " (Act 4:33)

The suggestion in this passage is that this event only pertained to The Twelve Apostles. However, it is probably best to say that the passage is ultimately inconclusive on the point. By the time Acts chapter four was written, there were probably several who had been given the bestowment of the Holy Spirit's power by the Apostles.

Many believers were given the ability to do signs wonders and mighty deeds. However, it is crucial to understand that they received these abilities through the ministry of The Twelve. They *alone* had the unique ability to impart a special "baptism" of the Spirit's presence that was revealed in miraculous occurrences.

Chapter 7

The Certification of the Twelve Apostles

*How To Know A Bona Fide Apostle
II Corinthians 12:11-12*

Our first church was nestled in a little village of 800 people in the middle of a blanket of cornfields in rural Michigan. Although it was not exactly country living, it was close. "Country" was a quarter mile in any direction from the center of town. Although we lived in the village, it was in that pastorate that I learned to hunt. Prior to that I had never hunted game, so I was "green" out in the field. I did not have a clue as to where to look or what to look for in reference to locating those elusive furry woodland creatures. After a few years of hunting, talking with hunters and consulting the sacred writ of hunters -- *Field and Stream Magazine* -- I learned that hunting required attentiveness to your surroundings. There were tell-tale signs for the discerning eye that revealed the presence of wildlife. Depending on the nature of the "sign", one could tell what kind of animal and even how recently that animal had been in a particular location.

"Sign" took a variety of forms. The most telling were paw or hoof prints. Sometimes there were markers where a buck (a male deer) had scraped a tree with his antlers. Shells along a stream or river indicated a raccoon. I remember seeing a small mass of fur, teeth and bones at the base of a tree. I later learned that owls swallow their prey whole and then regurgitate what is indigestible. Of course, kind and quantity of fecal droppings witness to what kind of creature walked the path that you have stepped in.

All in all, there are many signs in nature that tell us what something is, even if you cannot see the animal in question. The signs serve to identify the creature. After awhile, even the most inexperienced tenderfoot or city slicker can learn to interpret signs of wildlife. It is all a matter of knowing what to look for.

The Compelling Characteristics of Apostles

The Apostle Paul was ministering to a group of people that seemed to have trouble interpreting some signs that they should have been able to interpret. These signs he called the "signs of an apostle." He tells them that.

> "...Truly the signs of an apostle were wrought among you in all patience, in signs, and wonders, and mighty deeds." (II Corinthians 12:12)

The context of this statement by the Apostle Paul was the invasion of false teachers into the church at Corinth. They were trying to convince the believers there that the Apostle Paul was not really an Apostle after all. These false teachers had criticized and ridiculed Paul to the Corinthian believers and undermined his ministry to them. They were trying to convince the Corinthian believers that Paul was not really an authoritative Apostle!

Realizing that the relationship he had with them as well as the Gospel itself was in jeopardy, Paul, under inspiration, spends the majority of chapters 10-12 of II Corinthians telling them why they should continue to accept his leadership as an Apostle. He substantiated his authority over them in chapter 10. He details the superiority of his background over the false teachers in chapter 11. In chapter 12, he relates his own uniqueness as the recipient of wonderful revelations from God along with an accompanying "thorn" just to keep him humble (II Corinthians 12:7).

Now, some folks *like* to talk about themselves and their accomplishments. However, Paul was not comfortable at all in doing this. In these chapters, he feels forced to talk about himself in a way that seems to him to be foolish. However, his only purpose was to win back his place in the Corinthians' hearts and lives as an Apostle.

In II Corinthians 12:11 he seems to speak out of frustration. *"He* should not be commending himself to them!" he argues. *"They* should be commending him!" They should be testifying that he is an Apostle on a par with the chiefest Apostles, even though he does not personally think that he is so important.

> " I am become a fool in glorying; ye have compelled me: for I ought to have been commended of you: for in nothing am I behind the very chiefest apostles, though I be nothing." (II Corinthians 12:11)

Then he tells them why they should be commending him and his Apostleship: *They had observed first hand the characteristic signs of the presence of an Apostle.*

> **"Truly the signs of an apostle** were wrought among you in all patience, in signs, and wonders, and mighty deeds." (II Corinthians 12:12)

The Corinthian believers had seen Paul in full apostolic mode. Signs, wonders, and mighty deeds had been done among them in "all patience" (perseverance). The idea is that these signs were not just done once or twice. An abundance of these signs were done in their midst on a consistent, persistent basis. Paul is obviously surprised that there would even be a question among them about the matter of his apostleship when the evidence was so overwhelming. There should not have been any mistaking his right to be called an Apostle. Activities that *characterized, typified and identified* Apostles had been done by him repeatedly over a long period of time in their presence!

These significant statements about identifying an Apostle cannot be over emphasized! *The Apostle Paul is telling these believers that there were things done in their presence that only an Apostle could do!* These things identified *him* as an Apostle.

Everyone could not do what Paul had evidently done in their midst! He did things that only a select group could do. Since Paul did them, he argues, then they should realize that he was an Apostle just like the very chiefest Apostles. He is telling them to remember what he did and think about what his deeds clearly indicated -- *that he was an Apostle!*

This is an important truth that we need to focus upon. Grasping this truth will not only aid you in understanding what Paul says in II Corinthians 12, it will also help you to understand and interpret the religious world around you. What is being said in II Corinthians 12:11-12 is that there are certain things that Apostles did that identified them as Apostles. Paul said concerning himself, "I did the deeds that Apostles do. You should have recognized that. Why do I have to justify myself to you? The signs of an Apostle were so obviously performed in your presence that you should be endorsing *me*!"

All they had to do was follow the signs. And, reader, that is all you have to do as well. Once you know the signs of an Apostle, you will know an Apostle's unique abilities. Once you know an apostle's unique abilities, then you will have a profound clarity into not only the religious world around you, but your own walk with God as well.

What were the activities and abilities that identified who an Apostle was? II Corinthians 12:12 goes on to tell us that these identifying characteristics were revealed in "…. signs, and wonders, and mighty deeds."

Now, I am going to pause here for awhile because there is an important truth that I am not sure that the reader will grasp unless I focus in on it. What the Apostle Paul is saying is that *there are certain things that Apostles did that identified and confirmed the presence of an authentic Apostle of the Twelve variety. Paul said concerning himself, "I did the stuff that Apostles do."*

They should have recognized it. Why did he have to justify himself to them? The signs of an Apostle were so obviously performed in their presence that they should have been endorsing *him*! The things that follow, both in this passage and in other places, prove the apostleship of Paul. What was true for him had to be true of all the Apostles. Paul was citing the credentials that were true of *all* Apostles. Paul is claiming that the Lord Jesus chose him to be an Apostle in the same sense as the Twelve!

The Apostolic Credentials

It is important, in this discussion, to note that the Apostle Paul was claiming to be an Apostle, not in the generic sense described previously, but in the special sense that the Twelve were Apostles! There are five proofs of the Apostleship of Paul in the Scripture. Here are listed the credentials that were to be true of anyone claiming capital "A" apostolic office.

1. An Apostle was an independent witness to the resurrected Christ.

> In I Corinthians 9:1 Paul states: "Am I not an apostle? am I not free? **have I not seen Jesus Christ our Lord?** are not ye my work in the Lord?"

"Am I not free?" he asks, rhetorically. Although there may be an allusion to the contents of I Corinthians chapter eight in talking about Christian liberty, I believe Paul is, in fact, asserting his independence from the other Apostles even as they were independent from each other. He asserts that he had encountered the resurrected Jesus

Christ personally which was a prerequisite for Apostleship (Acts 1:22). In chapter 15 of I Corinthians, Paul relates how he was the last to see the resurrected Lord (Acts 9:1-6; I Corinthians 15:1-8) even stating that he was the last of all -- *the very last* -- as someone who was born past the due date.

> "And last of all he was seen of me also, as of one born out of due time." (I Corinthians 15:8)

He does not believe himself to be superior to the rest of the Apostles. In fact, he considers himself small. He is an Apostle nonetheless.

> "For I am the least of the apostles, that am not meet to be called an apostle, because I persecuted the church of God. But by the grace of God I am what I am: and his grace which was bestowed upon me was not in vain; but I labored more abundantly than they all: yet not I, but the grace of God which was with me." (I Corinthians 15:9-10)

2. An Apostle was personally commissioned by the Lord Jesus Christ.

Although Paul was not part of the original Twelve, his apostleship was decided at a level that is not subject to debate. As were the other Apostles, he was personally chosen by Jesus to fulfill that role. His choice as an Apostle was distinct from and different than the other Apostles, but no less valid.

> "Paul, an apostle, (not of men, neither by man, but by Jesus Christ, and God the Father, who raised him from the dead;)" (Galatians 1:1)

> "Paul, an apostle of Jesus Christ by the commandment of God our Savior, and Lord Jesus Christ which is our hope…" (1 Timothy 1:1)

Some Christians have asked whether the Apostles were premature or out of line in choosing Matthias in Acts one to make up the twelfth member of the team. Should they have waited? Was Paul *God's* choice to make up the twelfth member of the "Board of Directors"?

There is no biblical evidence to suggest that the Apostles were out of line in choosing Matthias to replace Judas, but the question remains: Where does that leave Paul?

It leaves him as an Apostle who was "born out of due time", specially chosen by the Lord for apostolic ministry. It leaves him as a witness of the resurrected Lord and one who gave abundant evidence in his life and ministry that he was chosen to be such (I Corinthians 15:8). He is not less in authority or ability than the others. He is simply in a separate category. He was especially chosen by the Lord for this office!

In his own defense, Paul gives to us the commonly accepted credentials that would make someone an Apostle.

3. An Apostle performed the characteristic events commonly associated with the Twelve Apostles.

"Truly the signs of an apostle were wrought among you in all patience, in **signs, and wonders, and mighty deeds**." (II Corinthians 12:12)

In the above passage, Paul states that he had performed the characteristic acts associated with the ministry of The Twelve. These indicators, he states to the Corinthians, should have been obvious to them. If being one of the Twelve was a disease, they should have been able to read the symptoms and drawn a conclusion! Let us take a few paragraphs to examine exactly what the Apostle Paul meant by the indicators (signs) of an Apostle.

Signs

Several signs are spoken of by the Lord Jesus Christ to the Apostles as the kinds of things that would mark their ministry. Mark 16 records the Lord Jesus Christ appeared to the (then) eleven Apostles after His resurrection but prior to Pentecost. He rebuked them for their unbelief and assured them that those that believed would have certain signature miraculous "signs" characterize their ministries. He gives them their commission to go into the world and preach. The miraculous signs would follow in the wake of their preaching ministry. Note the passage:

"Afterward he appeared unto the **eleven** as they sat at meat, and upbraided them with their unbelief and hardness of heart, because they believed not them which had seen him after he was risen. And he said unto them, Go ye into all the world, and preach the gospel to every creature. He that believeth and is baptized shall be saved; but he that believeth not shall be damned. And these signs shall follow them that believe; In my name shall they cast out devils; they shall speak with new tongues; They shall take up serpents; and if they drink any deadly thing, it shall not hurt them; they shall lay hands on the sick, and they shall recover." (Mark 16: 14-18) [1]

From this passage we can conclude that the signature events associated with their faith and ministry would be:

The ability to cast out demons (exorcism)

The ability to speak in languages they had not previously learned (tongues)

Immunity from deadly snake bites

Immunity from assassination by poison

The ability to heal the sick

Paul, we know, spoke in tongues, experienced these signs and apparently practiced them in front of the Corinthian believers. He said in 1 Corinthians 14:18... " I thank my God, I speak with tongues more than ye all". Paul had been bitten by a poisonous snake and was unaffected

---

[1] The author is aware that the presence of this passage is disputed among some textual scholars. Suffice to say that he does not believe that there is sufficient evidence to warrant its dispute.

(Acts 28:3-5). Paul and the other apostles had ministries wherein healings, exorcisms, tongues, and preservation from poison were typical (Acts 3:1-8; 9: 33-34; 14:8-10; 16:16-18).

Wonders and Mighty Deeds

Wonders and mighty deeds are categories of extraordinary events associated with the Twelve Apostles that Paul cites as being indicative of *his* apostolic status. These things are seen in the following extraordinary displays:

The death of Ananias and Saphira (Acts 5:1-11)

Peter's "shadow" healing (Acts 5:15-16)

Paul's "extended" ministry – miraculous events outside of his immediate presence but connected with him (Acts 19:11-12)

The raising of Dorcas and Eutychus from the dead (Acts 9:40-41; Acts 20:10)

Paul's defense to the Corinthian believers was that he had performed the same types of wonders and mighty deeds that were associated with the Twelve Apostles.

Possession of the Revelatory Gift

Though not mentioned in II Corinthians 12:12, Paul was a means through which the truth that the Lord Jesus promised was imparted. It has already been established that the Holy Spirit was promised to the Twelve Apostles to be the conduit of truth to them. They, in turn, imparted the truth given to them. Paul asserts:

> "Now **we** (the Apostles) have received, not the spirit of the world, but the spirit which is of God; that **we** (the Apostles) might know the things that are freely given to us of God. Which things also we (the Apostles) speak, not in the words which man's wisdom teacheth, but which the Holy Ghost teacheth; comparing spiritual things with spiritual."
> (1 Corinthians 2:12-13)

Even Peter compared the teachings of Paul to be on the level of the inspired Scripture.

> "And account that the longsuffering of our Lord is salvation; even as our beloved brother Paul also according to the wisdom given unto him hath written unto you; As also in all his epistles, speaking in them of these things; in which are some things hard to be understood, which they that are unlearned and unstable wrest, **as they do also the other scriptures**, unto their own destruction." (II Peter 3:15-16)

The Holy Spirit was given to be a conduit of truth from the Savior to His Apostles. The Apostles were promised this conduit of truth from the Lord Jesus. This function

---

(2) It is true that there were those other than Apostles who were used to impart revelation. Certainly, Mark and Luke are examples of those used to impart written revelation who were not Apostles. They were, however, in close association with them. Though it is not stated explicitly in Scripture that they possessed the baptism of the Spirit, they certainly had the prophetic gift indicating that this had indeed been given to them.

was directed to and distinctive of their ministry and was true of Paul as well.

3. An Apostle bestowed the baptism of the Spirit upon others.

As seen in a previous chapter, the Apostles possessed a unique ability to bestow the baptism of the Spirit. This baptism was an empowering presence of the Spirit of God that enabled the recipient to do various miraculous activities. Note that Paul had this ability as well.

> "And when Paul had laid his hands upon them, the Holy Ghost came on them; and they spake with tongues, and prophesied." (Acts 19:6)

This bestowal had been called the "gift of God." The writer believes that Paul is alluding to this impartation in admonishing Timothy *not* to be neglectful toward "...the gift of God, which is in thee **by the putting on of my hands**." (II Timothy 1:6)

Paul gave the "gift of God" to Timothy. This does not refer to salvation. This is a reference to the special impartation of the power of the Holy Spirit that apparently Paul had given to Timothy. How it was manifested in Timothy's life we are not told. We do know conclusively that it came from Paul's hands and that Paul had the ability, unique to the Twelve Apostles, of bestowing the power of the Spirit. He specifically tells Timothy to "stir up" this gift. The gift Timothy possessed was apparently latent in him but was not being actively implemented by him.

So here are the Apostolic credentials of Paul. He met five criteria to be considered one of the Twelve:

1. Paul was an independent witness to the resurrected Christ.
2. Paul was personally selected by the Lord Jesus Christ and the Father to be an Apostle (on a par with the Twelve).
3. Paul performed the characteristic events commonly associated with the Twelve.
4. Paul relayed revelatory prophecy.
5. Paul bestowed the baptism of the Spirit upon others.

This leads us back to our original text:

> "I am become a fool in glorying; ye have compelled me: for I ought to have been commended of you: for in nothing am I behind the very chiefest apostles, though I be nothing. Truly the signs of an apostle were wrought among you in all patience, in signs, and wonders, and mighty deeds."
> (II Corinthians 12:11-12)

Paul is telling these believers in Corinth that instead of him having to defend his Apostleship to them, they ought to be defending it before others. After all, they had witnessed the characteristic indicators that marked, authenticated and verified who was and who was not one of the "chiefest", the Twelve Apostles.

Chapter 8

The Termination of the Twelve Apostles

Are There Apostles Today?

Several years ago I was a pastor of a church in the metropolitan Detroit, Michigan area. One day I walked out of my office across the hall to my secretary's office to give her some work. I was only there for a short while. I turned around and was walking back to my office when I noticed a strange man standing there. His appearance was rather disheveled and he had a wild look in his eye. Although he did kind of fit in with the general decor, I was still a little surprised by his presence there. At the time the door was not latching properly, so I assumed that he just walked in. Anyway, I said to the guy, "May I help you?"

"Can I be John the Baptist?" he inquired. (Now that's a question you don't hear everyday).

I was not sure that I heard him right so I asked him what he said.

He asked once more, "Can I be John the Baptist?"

I thought it might be a trick question so I asked him slowly, "Are you asking me if *you* could be John the Baptist?

"Yes", he replied.

I said, "No"

"Why not?", he asked.

"Because he's dead!" I said with finality.

He just kind of stared at me and went on to some other lunacy. Eventually, I ushered him out of my office and out of the building.

But just for a moment let us entertain the thought -- *Could he really have been John the Baptist?!* Maybe he *was* John the Baptist raised from the dead and what more appropriate place for him to visit than a Baptist Church?! He did seem to appear out of nowhere....Hmmmm. Maybe I had been premature in just assuming he was mentally off. After all, John the Baptist wore camel's hair and ate locusts. This guy in my office was a little different, too. Maybe I should have at least been open to the idea that this strange man really was John the Baptist. I speak as a fool! John the Baptist was a man born for a particular purpose and calling unique to him.

The Twelve Apostles were also a unique, honored group as has already been established. They had a unique relationship with the Lord Jesus Christ. They were the means through which the Lord conveyed His truth through the Spirit to the world after He left it. They were given a special endowment of power that the Savior promised would be given them at Jerusalem on the day of Pentecost. They were also the means whereby dramatic displays of power were conveyed to those with whom they came in contact. They could convey the power of the

Holy Spirit to others to do miraculous signs and wonders such as speaking in other languages or healings.

This ability was especially unique to them. Though others could *receive* this power from them, those who received it could not give it to others. That ability was limited to the Apostles. This was what it meant to be one of that special group. Their role is not repeated nor is it duplicated. They were for a time and a season unique to them. As such, there are no Apostles today.

The Apostles Were Foundational

The New Testament book of Ephesians details the blessings of heaven that believers have in Christ (Ephesians 1:3). Among those blessings is the fact that Gentiles are a part of the household of God in Christ. We are part of God's temple built from a solid foundation. That foundation is that which came from Apostles and prophets.

> "Now therefore ye are no more strangers and foreigners, but fellowcitizens with the saints, and of the household of God; And are **built upon the foundation of the apostles and prophets**, Jesus Christ himself being the chief corner stone; In whom all the building fitly framed together groweth unto an holy temple in the Lord: In whom ye also are builded together for an habitation of God through the Spirit." (Eph 2:19-22)

The Twelve were foundational to the early church. Those in the household of God "are built upon the foundation of the apostles and prophets, Jesus Christ himself being the chief corner stone;" (Eph 2:20). The Twelve had a unique establishing role in the early Church. *A foundation for any building is laid only once.* The Church in its infancy needed these men and we reap today the fruit of their lives through their early ministries and the inspired Scriptures that they helped impart.

The Apostles Were Confirmational

The Apostles, with their unique distinction as personal witnesses to the resurrection of Jesus, were given abilities that were designed to confirm the message of salvation in Christ. The Scripture is very clear that the miraculous ministry they were given was designed to confirm that personal witness. The writer to the Hebrews confesses this truth as he instructs his readers to pay "earnest heed" to the message of salvation.

> "Therefore we ought to give the more earnest heed to the things which we have heard, lest at any time we should let them slip. For if the word spoken by angels was steadfast, and every transgression and disobedience received a just recompence of reward; How shall we escape, if we neglect so great salvation; which at the first began to be spoken by the Lord, **and was confirmed unto us by them that heard him;** (the Twelve) **God also bearing them** (the Twelve) **witness, both with signs and wonders, and with divers miracles, and gifts of the Holy Ghost, according to his own will?"**
> (Hebrews 2:1-4)

Note that verse four tells us that the message was "confirmed" by them that heard him.

How was this confirmed? It was confirmed by signs, wonders, miracles and gifts of the Holy Spirit. Those that heard Him were the Apostles who had been personal witnesses to Christ's earthly ministry. The miraculous events had the purpose of substantiating to those who had not seen the Lord that what these witnesses were saying was true.

A significant aspect of this is that the writer to the Hebrews did not say that the confirmation process was *still* happening in their midst. It happened in a time past done by those that had seen the Lord. It is apparent that the writer to the Hebrews is not alluding to present events or occurrences that were ongoing at the time of the writing of this letter to the Hebrews. The confirmation process had happened but was not currently happening. The witness of the message of salvation had already been confirmed and the Hebrews were warned about neglecting that message.

The Apostles were Transitional

The Apostle Paul had defended his Apostleship to the Corinthians. As has been already pointed out, one of the central qualifications of being an Apostle was to have been a witness of the resurrected Christ. Paul makes a point of saying that he had personally seen the resurrected Jesus in I Corinthian 15.

> "And last of all he was seen of me also, as of one born out of due time." (I Corinthians 15:8)

The above verse establishes that Paul had been witness to the resurrected Lord. It also points out another significant fact. Paul is saying that he was the "last of all" to see the resurrected Lord Jesus as one who was overdue. The idea being expressed is compared to a woman who was overdue in giving birth. He came later, but he came nonetheless; and he was the last of all to see the resurrected Lord. In other words, Paul is stating that no one else had seen the Lord in this way. He is saying that no one else who came after him could qualify. There are no more folks waiting in the wings. "Last of all" means no more coming. He was last in line.

This statement is significant from several standpoints. Someone claiming to be an Apostle on the level of the Twelve had to meet the criteria for one. One of those criteria was to have personally encountered the resurrected Lord.

> "Am I not an apostle? am I not free? have I not seen Jesus Christ our Lord?" (1 Corinthians 9:1)

Paul asserted that he is the *last* to have seen the Lord in this way. The implication is that since this was so, he was also the *last* of the Apostles. It is clear that since being a personal earthly witness to the resurrected Christ was essential to Apostolic ministry and since he was the last to have seen the Lord in this way, then there could be no one else to make this claim. There were no more Apostles coming after Paul.

The Apostles Were Terminal

We have seen that there are certain elements that were typical of the designated Twelve Apostles.

> They were people personally selected by the Lord for this position.
>
> They were personal witnesses to the resurrected Christ.
>
> They were recipients of a special power.
>
> They performed miraculous deeds indentifying them as the chosen Apostles.
>
> They possessed an unique ability to give the Holy Spirit's power in a special way, enabling others who were not Apostles to perform miraculous deeds.
>
> They were the conduit for truth from the Lord Jesus Christ to His people.

We have also seen that the Apostles' ministry was foundational and confirmational in nature. Paul has testified to the transitory nature of apostolic ministry in his assertion that he was the last to be able to qualify as seeing the resurrected Lord. The reality of life on this planet testifies to this as well.

"Because he's dead," was the answer I gave to my bizarre visitor who wondered if he could be John the Baptist. I had thought it was a good answer, though I did not think that it affected him much. Let me use this argument in reference to the apostles. Go ahead and ask me, "Could I be an Apostle?"

Answer: "No"

"Why not?"

Here it comes! Ready? "Because they're dead!" OK, maybe that was not dramatic enough. "The Apostles are dead, *dead , DEAD!"*

Now we know they are not dead in an eternal sense. We know that they are with the Lord. Paul said,

> "Therefore we are always confident, knowing that, whilst we are at home in the body, we are absent from the Lord: (For we walk by faith, not by sight:)
> We are confident, I say, and willing rather to be absent from the body, and to be present with the Lord." (II Corinthians 5:6-8)

Paul said that he was torn between staying in his earthly body and going to be with Christ (Philippians 1:20-23). We know that the Apostles are with the Lord, just as anyone who has admitted their sin and turned to the Savior is with the Lord at physical death. Those who have trusted the resurrected Savior in repentant faith, trusting only in His all sufficient payment for their sin on the cross to give them forgiveness, are assured of eternal life (John 3:16-18). Anyone who has trusted Christ in this way will be with Him throughout eternity.

However, friend, when we die our earthly ministries are over. When the Apostles completed their unique purposes for being here, they died as well. Like the New Testament prophets, they were foundational and transitional. Only the Lord Jesus has a continual, eternal ministry (Hebrews 7:25). We have already pointed out that the Twelve will have a future ministry in governance (Matthew 19:28; Luke 22:30; Revelation 21:14). We also know that those who know the Lord will reign with Him during the Millennium (Revelation 20:6). However, until that time, whether Apostles or "common" saints, no one is said to have any earthly ministries after they exit this life.

The apostolic ministry, including their abilities to do the miraculous and impart the miracle working power of the Holy Spirit, was a foundational, transitional office that the early church was given. When the Apostles passed off the scene, those aspects of their ministry that came directly from them ceased as well. This included the special baptism of the Spirit which was evidenced in the miraculous. Within a generation of the death of the Apostles, the miraculous events that were typical of the Apostolic age ceased as well. Those who received the baptism of the Spirit from the Apostles with their accompanying gifts eventually died. With their death went the distinctive *signs* of the ministry of the Apostles.

Reader, Paul knew that one day his ministry would be over. He said in Philippians that he had a desire to go be with Jesus. In II Corinthians chapter five he talks about being absent from the body and present with the Lord. The Apostle Paul went to be with his Savior.

Simon Peter and Andrew, James and John (the sons of Zebedee), Philip, Bartholomew, Thomas, Matthew, James (the son of Alphaeus), Thaddaeus (also called Lebbaeus), Simon the Canaanite, as well as Matthias, all went to be with the Savior. When they did so, their earthly ministry was over. Those men are all with the Lord Jesus. They were a select group with a special calling from God that they fulfilled. The last to die was John. When John left this world for that fairer land, the saturation of the miraculous that seemed to be typical in the early church ceased to be normal. This happened in less than a generation after his death.

My friend, I can say with finality that their task was completed when they entered the gates of Heaven and the Lord said, "Well done, thou good and faithful servant." There is no biblical proof that they have a current role. Any supposed ministry they continue to have with human beings on this earth today is the stuff of fables and superstition derived from paganism or vivid imaginations.

Today, there are various groups that claim to have the apostolic office preserved or reinstated in their movement. Roman Catholicism claims that the Pope occupies the chair (apostolic authority) of Saint Peter and that the authority of the Apostles rests within that church. Mormonism also lays claim to this authority. The Community of Christ (Reorganized Church of Latter Day Saints) claims this. Throughout history, there have been self-styled prophets and apostles prognosticating, pontificating and claiming the office of Apostle. These and others claim to have the authority of Apostles over their adherents. They often lay claim to being able to convey divine revelation as well. Their claims notwithstanding, it is evident that the apostolic office has ceased. It ended with the death of the last Apostle.

Reader, mark it down that any religious leaders claiming this kind of authority "...*are* false apostles, deceitful workers, transforming themselves into the apostles of Christ. And no marvel; for Satan himself is transformed into an angel of light. Therefore *it is* no great thing if his ministers also be transformed as the ministers of righteousness; whose end shall be according to their works." (II Corinthians 11: 13-15).

There was a popular science fiction TV series on years ago called "Star Trek". The doctor, known as "Bones", seemed to have one line he said in various ways in almost every episode. This line was "He's dead, Jim." "The Apostles are dead, Jim," and that is not bad news. That is the way it is supposed to be.

Frank I. Snyder

Chapter 9

The Legacy of the Twelve Apostles

"And they continued steadfastly in the apostles' doctrine..." (Acts 2:42)

*"The B – I – B – L – E!
Yes, That's The Book for Me!"*

It was 1971. I was young, barely 15 years old. I had only been a believer for a very short time. It is difficult to describe the sense of wonder at forgiveness and salvation in Jesus Christ that I had. It seemed that everything that I was hearing was like cold water on a hot, dry day. Truths that many believers grow up hearing about, I was hearing with virgin ears. Looking back, it was indeed wonderful.

Most new Christians can relate to what I am saying. I can remember when I found out about the Second Coming of Christ. Wow! (I mean, "Praise the Lord!") I was just glad He came the first time! I was like a sponge. In my wonder and enthusiasm I wanted to know everything that could be known of God and experience everything that could be experienced with God.

Hindsight and maturity now tell me that where I was then is the most vulnerable time in a new Christian's life. It is the time when doctrinal and theological foundations are being laid. It is a time when most young believers are looking to others for guidance and mentoring. It is also the time when they are most susceptible to religious ideas that may not be orthodox. That is where I was in 1971.

It was during this time of my life that I was told about an experience that could enhance my Christian life. I was told to get alone and begin to pray to God. As I prayed I was to begin to allow my mouth and my tongue to verbalize any syllables that might come out. I did not have to be saying understandable words because what was going to come out of my mouth was going to be a heavenly, angelic language. I was told that as I started to speak these syllables that the language would come out on its own. This, I was told, would be the gift of "tongues".

I went up to my room and knelt down and began to pray. Then I started to verbalize syllables and let out the "heavenly language" that I was told would be such a blessing in my life. As I began to do this, I realized that nothing was happening except I was forcing myself to speak gibberish. I got up off my knees, a little perplexed that nothing had "happened."

Overall, I cannot say that I was *too* troubled. At the time my attitude was, "Oh well, if God wants me to have this, He will give it to me." It was not a crisis event. It did not start a quest for the craved experiential encounter with God upon which some people embark. I must admit that I have reflected many times upon that evening. In some respects, it did influence me. It steered me toward my Bible. I have wondered since then that if something *had* happened that evening, would it have changed my perspective? The question is moot at this point. Even if it had changed my perspective, it would not mean that it *should* have done so.

The book of Acts records in chapter two verse 42 that the believers "continued steadfastly in the apostles' doctrine....." The Apostles' greatest gift to the believers was the doctrine (the teaching) that they imparted. Indeed, it was the doctrine embodied in the New Testament Scriptures, along with the Old Testament Scriptures, that were the priority with them. The miraculous manifestations they could enact or impart paled in importance to that.

Predicting the entrance of false teachers and prophets Paul warned Timothy that "...evil men and seducers shall wax worse and worse, deceiving, and being deceived." (II Tim. 3:13). Paul's main concern was that the doctrine that Timothy had learned be preserved. He admonishes Timothy to ..."continue thou in the things which thou hast learned and hast been assured of, knowing of whom thou hast learned *them"* (II Tim. 3:14). He tells Timothy to put his trust in the Scriptures alone.

> "And that from a child thou hast known the holy scriptures, which are able to make thee wise unto salvation through faith which is in Christ Jesus. All scripture *is* given by inspiration of God, and *is* profitable for doctrine, for reproof, for correction, for instruction in righteousness: That the man of God may be perfect, throughly furnished unto all good works." (II Timothy 3:15-16)

The Apostle John writes concerning doctrine:

> "Whosoever transgresseth, and abideth not in the doctrine of Christ, hath not God. He that abideth in

the doctrine of Christ, he hath both the Father and the Son. If there come any unto you, and bring not this doctrine, receive him not into *your* house, neither bid him God speed: For he that biddeth him God speed is partaker of his evil deeds." (II John 9-11)

Jude admonishes:

> "Beloved, when I gave all diligence to write unto you of the common salvation, it was needful for me to write unto you, and exhort *you* that ye should earnestly contend for the faith which was once delivered unto the saints." (Jude 3)

How different from many modern believers that look to an experience or to some self-styled prophet or apostle, rather than to a body of truth, for certainty and direction in this life! Paul's admonition to the Galatian believers is especially pertinent.

> "I marvel that ye are so soon removed from him that called you into the grace of Christ unto another gospel: Which is not another; but there be some that trouble you, and would pervert the gospel of Christ. But though we, or an angel from heaven, preach any other gospel unto you than that which we have preached unto you, let him be accursed. As we said before, so say I now again, If any *man* preach any other gospel unto you than that ye have received, let him be accursed." (Galatians 1:6-9)

Doctrine is paramount. Experience is irrelevant.

Should Experience Change Theology?

Right now I can almost guarantee that there are readers who are saying to themselves, "That Snyder guy is just wrong. I know what I have experienced, seen, felt, etc." There are multitudes of professed believers who claim to have experienced the baptism of the Holy Spirit of the Pentecostal variety. There are many sincere believers that truly believe that they have spoken in tongues. There are believers that are convinced that they have prophesied under the control of the Spirit of God. There are folks that believe that someone has laid their hands on them and they were healed or that they have laid hands upon someone and performed a miraculous healing. There are folks who have visited a shrine, drank miracle spring water, or received a prayer cloth from a "prophet" and will testify to receiving a healing, an epiphany or an unexpected financial windfall at the behest or touch of someone claiming divine power.

Still, experience does not change doctrine.

In almost 40 years of my Christian walk I have found that many, if not most, believers have mixed authorities in their lives as to decision-making and what they believe is true about God. The tendency in many circles is to have theology by anecdote and experience rather than by Scripture. "I saw this... I felt that... this happened, therefore, God is working." If something turned out well, then the supposition is that it was the will of God. If it did not turn out so well, then we must have gotten ahead of God's will for our lives. If one has an emotional feeling of peace, then it is concluded that it is God's will. If someone has an inexplicable recovery from an illness, then it must have been a miraculous healing from God. The idea is that "since certain events happened a certain way, therefore this is what must be true about God and His working."

Ultimately from this perspective, emotional and circumstantial experience becomes a primary authority if not *the* primary authority in a believer's life. The Scripture tends to be interpreted through the lens of experience, rather than the reverse. When experience is elevated to such an authoritative level, Scripture tends to be read with a subjective, mystical perspective.

At times someone will say, "I was reading the Bible and this is what it said *to me*." This kind of statement reveals that the one speaking interprets Scripture through an experiential lens. My response to that statement is always with a question, "What would that passage of Scripture say if *you* were not around?" Scripture cannot mean what it never meant. Its meaning is not determined by our circumstances, emotions or desires. Scripture should be understood by the historical, cultural and grammatical context in which God gave it.

Granted that there are legitimate interpretational differences in Scripture that sincere believers may have. We often disagree about what the Bible says. However, one's personal experience and emotional feelings are irrelevant to what it says. When feelings or events become authoritative or even highly influential, we will find ourselves on dangerous ground and susceptible to falsehood. Experience must not trump theology. But it often does in believers' lives. How does this elevation of experience happen?

Because of Discouragement and Despondency

Many sincere Christians have testified that the primary reason they have sought what has been called the "baptism" was a dryness or discouragement in their spiritual life. I admire one woman's honesty when she admitted that it was because of her *"desperation, and dryness, not because of my understanding, I began to seek this baptism of the Holy Spirit."*[1] Guy Chevreau, formerly a Baptist preacher, sought out what is considered to be the most radical aspect of the Pentecostalist movement -- the so-called "Toronto Blessing". He testified that he sought it out *"too desperate to be critical."* Southern Baptist evangelist, James Robison, in a spiritual crisis, sought out a charismatic to lay hands on him. [2]

At the root of much of this fascination with the supposed working of the Holy Spirit, related in especially Pentecostal/charismatic circles, is the fact that many professed believers are unsatisfied with their Christian lives!

---

[1] Jensen, Jerry, *Baptists and the Baptism of the Holy Spirit* Full Gospel Businessmen's Fellowship International 836 S. Figueroa St. Los Angeles 17, CA 1963 p.31

[2] Cloud, David Friday Church News Notes, March 7, 2006 Fundamental Baptist Information Service, P.O. Box 610368, Port Huron, MI www.wayoflife.org fbns@wayoflife.org

Certainly, there are periods of despondency, sometimes prolonged, that believers throughout history have encountered. We want deliverance from them. There are times when we feel doubtful and uncertain. We do not like that. Because of negative circumstances or events in our lives, we begin to seek a mystical experience with God. Truth be told, we would rather walk by sight than by faith. (Compare II Corinthians 5:7.) People are seeking a reality that goes beyond the boundaries of faith. They may claim that they do not wish to physically "see" God. However, the next best thing is to be able to "feel" God either physically or emotionally.

Because of Boredom

Many believers are bored in their Christian lives. The routine and humdrum of life and even the disciplines of the Christian life can add a degree of mediocrity at times. The sense of wonder about the things of God is absent from their lives. When someone assures them that the same miracle working that was typical of the apostolic age is for them, they long for it. In the course of seeking it, many enter a world of bizarre religious ideas and activities characterized by emotional extremes. The emotions experienced become validating witnesses of the divine source of the activity. Therein is danger.

There is danger in interpreting the emotional reactions that are often found in religious movements, revivals or awakenings and attributing them automatically to the empowerment of the Holy Spirit. The activities, responses and emotionalism are read into the Scripture rather than letting the Scripture speak for itself. Even adherents to the Pentecostal/charismatic movement register concern about the nature of what is going on in their midst. They question: *"what <are> these reports of extreme emotional reactions and unusual behavior currently observed around the world among Christians of various theological persuasions- reports of great weeping or laughter, shaking, extreme terror, visions, falling (or what is sometimes called being 'slain in the Spirit'), being drunk with the Spirit and other revival experiences? Something is certainly going on, and that something seems potent. Is it revival? Is it sent from God? ...We must be cautious in evaluating new religious movements. "*[3]

A Scripture Based or Experience Based Theology?

One leading proponent of charismatic theology, John Wimber, stated that he has "talked with many evangelical theologians who have undergone significant changes in their theology because of an experience."[4] From the research this writer has done, it would seem that this is the case for many that have sought and found an experience.

Many of the books written about what has been alternately called "the baptism", "the anointing", "the empowering" consist primarily of anecdotes and personal testimonies of people who have had unusual or supra-

---

[3] White, John *When The Spirit Comes With Power* Intervarsity Press, Downers Grove, Illinois 60515 1988. Pp.17-18

[4] Horton, Michael Scott, *Power Religion: The Selling Out of the Evangelical Church,* Chicago, Moody Press p. 78

natural experiences. Stories from the past or the present are submitted to "prove" the validity of the experience. Those that do not buy into it or question the accounts are accused of being *"blinded by preconceived traditions!"*[5]

One seeker of "the baptism" sought out an evangelist who was said to impart the supernatural power of the Spirit. After at least one failed attempt, the evangelist struck the seeker's hands. An associate who described the encounter said that, "John fell again. But this time he dialed down a lot of the analysis and said, 'I don't care, I'm just going to take what God has to give.' When he quit analyzing what was occurring, he began experiencing the manifestations typical of the radical aspects of the 'charismatic' movement. This man later claimed that one of the biggest hindrances to receiving this experience was 'fear of deception.'" [6]

Wimber's encounters with those theologians is typical of what happens in many believers' lives. Experience becomes the primary means of interpreting what the Scripture says rather than letting the text speak. The experience evaluates the text rather than the text validating the experience. However, as Michael Horton observes, "shifts in one's theology ought to be motivated

---

[5] Jensen, Jerry, *Baptists and the Baptism of the Holy Spirit* Full Gospel Businessmen's Fellowship International 836 S. Figueroa St. Los Angeles 17, CA 1963 p.31

[6] Cloud, David Friday Church News Notes, March 24, 2006 Fundamental Baptist Information Service, P.O. Box 610368, Port Huron, MI www.wayoflife.org fbns@wayoflife.org

by a change of mind that has come about after careful reflection on the meaning of Scripture. Our experiences are never sufficient in overturning theological convictions we claim to have derived from the text itself…If we cannot think critically, logically, or rationally and arrive at our conclusions on the basis of objective facts rather than subjective experiences, the authority of Scripture is effectively undermined, regardless of how firmly one insists he or she maintains it."[7]

Sometimes someone will tell me about some strange event that happened to them or some supposed communication from "the other side". They look at me as if they want my validation or respect. They have had some sort of experience that was real to *them*. My response is that the teaching of Scripture remains unchanged.

Proponents of what is claimed to be "the baptism of the Holy Spirit" say that it has profoundly affected their lives, their perspective of the Christian life, and their understanding of Scripture. In many cases, the personal experience supersedes the authority and plain statements of Scripture. To such folks, the contents of this book will be summarily dismissed because it contradicts or does not reinforce their religious experience. Therein is a big problem. When personal experience is elevated, the Bible ceases to be authoritative in and of itself.

Several years ago I realized that in many Christians' lives, the Bible was not the only source for truth and

---

[7] Ibid. Horton, p. 79

guidance from and about God. Many believers embrace the Scriptures *and* a kind of mysticism as the leading authority in their Christian lives. While acknowledging the inspiration and authority of the Bible, they also identify the "leading of the Holy Spirit" as a major factor, if not *the* leading factor in their daily lives. I certainly do not want to be dismissive of the fruit-bearing and convicting work of the Spirit. However, many are claiming to possess the prophetic gift that was the result of the baptism imparted by The Twelve.

I want to add that I do not believe that there is deviousness or insincerity among them. My point is that "the woods is full" of these kinds of believers who accept extra-biblical authority, wacky ideas and practices without discernment. Because of this, heresy is rampant and falsehood prevails.

At the time of this writing, a Pentecostal evangelist by the name of Todd Bentley has been conducting meetings. This writer has personally observed Bentley kicking a man in the stomach because, he claimed, "God told him to". On another occasion I observed Bentley, a very large man run full-speed across a stage and bowl over another person seeking a healing, again, because "God" told him to. Bentley has claimed that God has told him to do these and other violent acts in his ministry. The sad aspect of this is that multitudes of people have believed him and flocked to his meetings. His ministry has been replete with bizarre actions and claims. Yet he has had a large constituency at his meetings which were broadcast on GOD TV.

Recently this same evangelist separated from his wife after admitting an inappropriate relationship with a female co-worker and use of alcohol. His meetings are presently suspended and he has since resigned from the ministry that he founded. His fall has shaken the charismatic world. On the heels of Bentley's fall, the editor of *Charisma* magazine, J. Lee Grady, asked, "Why do so many people flock to Lakeland from around the world to rally behind an evangelist who had serious credibility issues from the beginning?" His conclusion was that the charismatic movement was "just plain gullible." Grady, referring to his charismatic brethren, went further and observed, "Many of us would rather watch a noisy demonstration of miracles, signs and wonders than have a quiet Bible study. Yet we are faced with the sad reality that our untempered zeal is a sign of immaturity. Our adolescent craving for the wild and crazy makes us do stupid things. It's way past time we grew up."[8]

Grady stated that a Pentecostal evangelist related to him, "I'm now convinced that a large segment of the charismatic church will follow the anti-Christ when he shows up because they have no discernment."[9]

Now, I would not agree with that evangelist's eschatology. Neither do I agree that the problem is simply a lack of discernment. Grady attributes the tendency of

---

[8] Grady, J Lee *Charisma,* charismag.com acc. 8/13/08

[9] Ibid.

charismatics to fall for deception such as Bentley's to gullibility and/or spiritual immaturity. However, the central cause of this chaos is a flawed understanding of what the Bible teaches about the apostolic baptism of the Holy Spirit. It is the placing of experience above the authority of the Word of God.

I recall a conversation that occurred almost 40 years ago with some folks who were experience-oriented. They said to me, *"If you say this is not of God, you will go straight to hay'll."*

There were two significant aspects to this statement. First, I had never heard the word "hell" expressed as a two-syllable word before. That was interesting. The second aspect of the experience was the threat of perdition if there was any question as to the legitimacy of what they practiced in the name of God. Since that time, I have encountered many folks that attribute many different kinds of activities to the Holy Spirit of God. Those of us who are skeptical are not allowed to question the source or the reality of the experience for two primary reasons:

1. We have not experienced it, so how can we question it?

2. They *have* experienced it and *know* it is from God, therefore it *is* from God and we will be blaspheming the Holy Sprit if we say it isn't so.

Argument over! Experience reigns. Be silent no matter how bizarre the activity, no matter how much damage to the cause of Christ, no matter how far afield biblically someone goes.

However, *"the heart is deceitful"* says the prophet, *"and desperately wicked"* (Jeremiah 17:9). *"There is a way which seemeth right unto a man, but the end thereof are the ways of death"* (Proverbs 14:12). People can be deceived in their feelings, interpretations of circumstances and events. Often our own personal desires influence our understanding. What we want or feel can sway us as we interpret not only God's Word but His working in our lives or the lives of others. Feelings of peace or excitement validate our experiences and cause believers to fall for the Todd Bentleys of this world. Sadly, Bentley may be gone but there will be a parade of others that will take his place and a multitude will follow them. Dear reader, do not be one of them!

The Apostles were Jesus' conduit for truth to us. They imparted a body of truth from Jesus to His followers. What we have of that truth is in the New Testament. That is the Apostles' doctrine that we are to continue steadfastly in.

God does not impart the baptism of the Holy Spirit as He did at Pentecost. Only the Apostles received the ability to impart that power of the Spirit. He does not *gift* people to do signs, wonders, and mighty deeds as He did in the early church. God is no longer imparting revelation. The prophetic gift was for a time and a season imparted through the ministration of the Spirit by the Apostles.

That does not mean that God cannot do wondrous things or that, on occasion, will not do something remarkable. However, there is no evidence from Scripture that anyone is gifted to do a miracle ministry. Anyone who claims such is claiming a special calling or office from God for this. Scripture is plain that no office was forthcoming after the last of the Apostles had died. There is no hint in Scripture that the apostolic office was passed down to anyone. Certainly no one has met nor could meet the criteria for an Apostle in the sense that the Twelve fulfilled this role. There were Apostle-shaped holes in the early church that only they could fill.

Chapter 10

Life in the Post-Apostolic Age

Christian Living in the Absence of Apostles

I am sure that there are many who think that this writer is saying that since the ministry of the Twelve is over and the special endowment of the Spirit they imparted is done that God does nothing miraculous or extraordinary in this age. Such could not be further from the truth! There have been many occasions when this author and his wife have experienced the provision and intervention of God. Prayer has been answered and God has proven Himself many times.

There have been providential workings of God in our lives and in the lives of our church folks. It is to the point that I *expect* Him to work providentially and am not surprised when He does. I believe that God still heals people in answer to prayer in accordance with His sovereign working. I have witnessed many "coincidences" that are too coincidental to be purely coincidence. Suffice to say that I believe in an active, personal, powerful God!

However, friend, there is a big distinction between acknowledging a prayer-hearing and active God and believing that a miraculous era that was typical of the first century must be normative for every age or for this present age. From a practical aspect of Christian living we must ask ourselves: **What is normative for this age?**

The question naturally comes that if what was typical of the early church is not the norm for today, then what can we expect today? To ascertain what is normal today we must reflect upon what was normative then. By *normative* we mean what was the typical, average, common, usual, prevalent, regular, standard conduct or behavior whereby one could tell that a person had this divine empowerment? What was typical then that is not typical now?

Remember, it is the conclusion of this author that:

- The manifestation of power, called the "gift of God" (Acts 8:20; II Tim 1:6), demonstrated at Pentecost (Acts 2:1-4), and among the Gentile converts (Acts 10:44-48) is not for this age. It was a unique one time event in biblical history.

- This ability to impart this phenomenon known as the "gift of God" was limited to the Twelve Apostles.

In determining what is normal for today it is crucial to recognize what was normal during the apostolic age.

<u>All</u> the Believers the Apostles Encountered Were Given This Special Gift of the Holy Spirit

1. It was given to <u>all</u> the believers in Samaria:

"Now when the apostles which were at Jerusalem heard that Samaria had received the word of God, they sent unto them Peter and John: Who, when they were come down, prayed for them, that they might receive the Holy Ghost: (For as yet he was fallen upon none of them: only they were baptized in the name of the Lord Jesus.) Then laid they *their* hands on them, and they received the Holy Ghost." (Acts 8:14-17)

2. It was given to <u>all</u> the Gentile believers in Acts 10:

"While Peter yet spake these words, the Holy Ghost fell on all them which heard the word."(Acts 10:44)

3. It was given to <u>all</u> the believers in Acts 19:

"He said unto them, Have ye received the Holy Ghost since ye believed? And they said unto him, We have not so much as heard whether there be any Holy Ghost. And he said unto them, Unto what then were ye baptized? And they said, Unto John's baptism. Then said Paul, John verily baptized with the baptism of repentance, saying unto the people, that they should believe on him which should come after him, that is, on Christ Jesus. When they heard *this*, they were baptized in the name of the Lord Jesus. And when Paul had laid *his* hands upon them, the Holy Ghost came on them; and they spake with tongues, and prophesied."(Acts 19:2-6)

4. It was apparently given to <u>all</u> the Corinthian believers :

"But the manifestation of the Spirit is given to every **(each)** man to profit withal. For to one is given by the

Spirit the word of wisdom; to another the word of knowledge by the same Spirit; To another faith by the same Spirit; to another the gifts of healing by the same Spirit; To another the working of miracles; to another prophecy; to another discerning of spirits; to another *divers* kinds of tongues; to another the interpretation of tongues: But all these worketh that one and the selfsame Spirit, dividing to every man severally as he will." (I Corinthians 12:7-11)

This divine empowerment was apparently given by the Twelve Apostles to all who believed and its possession was accompanied by various miraculous occurrences such as prophecy and tongues, the spirit of wisdom, word of knowledge, gift of faith, gifts of healing, the ability to do miracles, etc. Apparently, all believers had one or more of these abilities as a result of the reception of the Spirit through the ministry of the Apostles.

Gifts such as tongues, prophecy, words of knowledge, and healing gifts appear to be normative in the early church. Indeed, the gift of tongues seemed to be the "clincher" -- the proof that believers possessed this empowerment. Note following passages:

> "And they were all filled with the Holy Ghost, and **began to speak with other tongues**, as the Spirit gave them utterance. " (Acts 2:4)

> "While Peter yet spake these words, the Holy Ghost fell on all them which heard the word. And they of the circumcision which believed were astonished, as many as came with Peter, because that on the

Gentiles also was poured out the gift of the Holy Ghost. **For they heard them speak with tongues**, and magnify God. Then answered Peter, 'Can any man forbid water, that these should not be baptized, which have received the Holy Ghost as well as we?'" (Acts 10:44-47)

"And when Paul had laid *his* hands upon them, the Holy Ghost came on them; **and they spake with tongues**, and prophesied." (Acts 19:16)

The Baptism of the Spirit and Accompanying Miraculous Displays Are Not Normative For Today

Since these miraculous abilities were the normal evidence of the empowerment of the Holy Spirit, and since this empowerment was given only by Apostles, then it follows that these miraculous kinds of activities ceased to be normative after the first Christians passed off the scene. Thus, divinely-gifted individuals are not in the church today, having ended when the last gifted individual passed into the Lord's presence probably early in the second century. Therefore, miraculous healings through the word or touch of *gifted* individuals are not normative for today and no one should be claiming them as such. This leads us to the conclusion that the following are not to be considered normal for believers in this day:

-The ability to speak in previously unknown languages (tongues) *as a gift* is not normative today.

-The ability to interpret tongues is not possessed *as a gift* by anyone today.

-The prophetic gift, in the sense of receiving and delivering new revelation, is no longer manifest today.

-The ability to do "miracle working" in general is not possessed by anyone today.

-None of the miraculous manifestations that accompanied the empowerment of the Spirit are normative for today.

Please understand, it is not that God *cannot* do the miraculous or extraordinary. It is that He *does not* bestow the abilities to individuals to do the miraculous or extraordinary. Those abilities were the outworking of the baptism of the Spirit that was bestowed by the Apostles. This occurrence was for a time and a season and for a specific reason. God does not do this today. Saying this is not a lack of faith. It is a recognition of a biblical reality.

Walking by Faith and Manifesting Spiritual Fruits are Normative for Today

It is beyond the scope of this book to deal extensively with the Spirit-filled life and its associated fruits (Galatians 5:22-25). It is also beyond the scope of this book to spend a great deal of time on the process of sanctification that the Holy Spirit effects in believers' lives through the renewing of the mind (Romans 12:1-2). Suffice to say that the filling of (walking in) the Spirit is a command to and achieved *by* believers (Ephesians 5:18; Galatians 5:16)) whereas the special endowment (baptism) of the Spirit was done *to* believers. The first is an act of obedience by believers, the second was a gift bestowed upon believers by the Apostles.

The Spirit's presence and work in believers in this age is supposed to be witnessed in a transformed life. "For the fruit of the Spirit is in all goodness and righteousness and truth" (Ephesians 5:9) as opposed to what is characteristic of the lost world around us. It is supposed to be manifested in the "love, joy, peace, longsuffering, gentleness, goodness, faith, meekness, (and) temperance" (Galatians 5:22-23) that come by walking in the Spirit.

What About Those Who Claim Otherwise?

There are those that have made the claim that God healed them or provided for them in some remarkable way. To this I say, "Praise the Lord!" However, if they are attributing these occurrences to some individual who claims to have the baptism of the Spirit and somehow caused, affected or aided them in their healing, this did not happen. No one possesses that ability today. No one possesses the baptism of the Spirit today. No one has the ability to do miracles today. No one possesses a healing ministry today. No one has the ability to impart the special endowment of the Spirit.

There are also those that say that they have received the baptism of the Spirit and then spoken in an unknown tongue. To that I say, "No, you didn't! You did not receive the baptism of the Spirit, nor did you speak in tongues as a result. Why? Because you would have had to receive such from an original Apostle and that did not happen. Therefore, you could not have spoken, prayed, sung or babbled in tongues!"

This writer is *not* saying that God cannot enable someone to speak in a language he had never learned. Nor is he saying that God cannot enable someone to understand a language he has never studied. Certainly, God is **able** to do these things! However, He is not giving anyone a *gift* of tongues or a *gift* of interpreting that they possess and use at will. That was what was happening in the New Testament church.

Then what, you may ask, is happening among multitudes of seemingly sincere Christians? What about the claims of miraculous events taking place? What about those that claim that there have been waves of the moving of the Spirit over various generations since the early 1900's? What about the very strange practices that often go on?

I do not pretend to understand all the dynamics that go on within religious movements as a whole or in particular churches. Over the centuries there were periods of religious movements and stirrings. These were sometimes called *awakenings* or *spiritual revivals.* Sometimes very strange and bizarre behavior occurred such as people barking like dogs, howling, falling over, writhing on the floor in delirium or laughing like hyenas.

Excitement sometimes escalated into hysteria. They claimed to experience euphoric joy. It was often claimed that miraculous occurrences accompanied these religious movements. They also claimed it was God-induced, though often there was very serious doctrinal error being spread in the course of these so-called revivals.

Even today, the so-called charismatic renewal unites very different theological persuasions around a common religious experience such as tongues. There are Catholic charismatics and Mormon charismatics as well as *Bapticostals*. Because of an experience they share (usually what they call "tongues") theologically contradictory groups are setting aside the tenets of their faith in view of their common experience.

I remember as a young lad walking past a church in our town that some called a *holy roller* church. I never went in but I would stand and listen from outside and hear the shouts and screams coming from inside. I did not understand it then and I still do not. I do not *have* to either understand it or explain the myriad of claims and practices that parade down the religious pike. I do not have to experience them either. All that I must do is "rightly divide the word of truth" (II Timothy 2:15).

The word of truth tells me that those miraculous gifts that were markers of the ministry of the Twelve Apostles are not extant in this age, despite the claims of the deliberately dishonest, the honestly deceived or the sincerely devout.

With that said, I also say that this same God who is capable of doing anything that He wishes, chooses the time and seasons in which He works and through whom He works. Even in biblical history there was not a continuous stream of the miraculous. There were clusters of miraculous events associated with particular people and circumstances in biblical history. Moses and Joshua, the Judges, Elijah and Elisha, Daniel, the Lord Jesus Christ and His Apostles -- all of these occupied a rather short time frame compared to the overall scope of biblical history. Out of some 6,000 years of biblical history, there was perhaps only 150 years where spectacularly miraculous events were taking place. Even then, the events were exceptional, not typical. Yet there are those claiming that miraculous events are to be the norm for this age. These occurrences have never been the norm in the past and are not so today!

I realize the difficulty for some folks to accept this. Some readers may currently be or may have been involved in the excited activity and spiritual intrigue of the Pentecostal/charismatic movement and its leaders. For them to admit that the apostolic baptism of the Holy Spirit was only for a specific age would seem to be a repudiation of their past or present involvement in that movement. It would perhaps even lead to questioning the validity of their own personal experiences. It is a difficult spot to be in, indeed!

There are those that are truly afraid that what is in this book is true. To accept it would, for them, mean that we are not left with much in our Christianity. But what *are* we left with if apostolic ministry is not typical or normative for this age?

What we Have

We still have a God who answers the prayer of faith in accordance with His own will. We are left with the knowledge of the glory of God in the face of Jesus Christ (II Corinthians 4:6). We are left with "the love of Christ, which passeth knowledge, that ye might be filled with all the fullness of God" (Ephesians 3:19). We are left with the Word of God that is quick and powerful and sharper than any two edged sword (Hebrews 4:12), that performs its work in our lives and carves, shapes and transforms us into the image of the Savior (Romans 12:1-2). We have the regenerating power of the Holy Spirit who can make spiritually dead men and women and boys and girls alive in Christ (John 3:3; Ephesians 2:1-5). We have the Lord Jesus Christ and His merciful grace on Calvary, His triumph over the grave, assurance of salvation in Him and the knowledge of dwelling with Him forevermore. We have *Him* and *He*, my friend, is enough!

> "For this cause I bow my knees unto the Father of our Lord Jesus Christ, Of whom the whole family in heaven and earth is named, That he would grant you, according to the riches of his glory, to be strengthened with might by his Spirit in the inner man; That Christ may dwell in your hearts by faith; that ye, being rooted and grounded in love, May be able to comprehend with all saints what is the breadth, and length, and depth, and height; And to know the love of Christ, which passeth knowledge, that ye might be filled with all the fullness of God. Now unto him that is able to do exceeding abundantly above all that we ask or think, according to the power

that worketh in us,   Unto him be glory in the church by Christ Jesus throughout all ages, world without end. Amen." (Ephesians 3:14-21)

Appendix One

Two Exceptions to the Rule

*Apparent Inconsistencies Regarding
the Impartation of the Spirit's Power*

We do not like exceptions in the Bible. We like consistency and uniformity. When practices are not done or words are not used the same way in every context, we grow anxious and stressed. We wonder how we can know anything for sure in interpreting Scripture! Friend, we have to cope with these things in Scripture just the way we cope with them in life. Every parent realizes that one deals differently with a child who deliberately breaks something as opposed to one that accidently breaks something. The outcome may be the same -- a broken object -- but the response should be different. Much of life has to cope with exceptions and contingencies.

For several years, this writer has served as a police chaplain. In the course of accompanying officers one learns that circumstances and intent are two major considerations in dealing with people. For example, one evening while riding with an officer, we received a radio report from a neighboring community of a drunk driver heading our way. We observed a car driving erratically. People were honking and giving hand signals to us that there was a drunk driver in a small white car ahead of them. Indeed, the driver had run a red light and had nearly collided with other drivers. The behavior of the vehicle would indicate that the driver was, in fact, drunk and that an arrest was going to happen.

We pulled the driver over and found that the lady inside was an elderly person that had just been released from the hospital that day. She was confused and disoriented and responded in a dazed manner. Emergency medical people were called and it was found that her blood sugar had bottomed out and she was disoriented. She had been driving around looking for her home since mid afternoon and it was now about 10:00 p.m. Even though she had violated several traffic laws and endangered others, she was not arrested. Because of the circumstances, she was instead cared for and sent to the hospital. Under other circumstances the same behavior would have gotten her arrested and sent to jail. Exceptions and contingencies are part of life.

As we have already seen, Paul himself was an exception to the apostolic order. That was at issue in Corinth -- the exceptional nature of Paul's apostleship. The author has maintained in this book that the role of the Apostles was crucial in the early church especially as related to the impartation of the empowering presence of the Holy Spirit known as *the baptism of the Holy Spirit*. It has been established that "...through the laying on of the apostles' hands that the Holy Ghost was given"(Acts 8:18). That was the general procedure. Yet there are two major exceptions to that normal procedure.

Exception #1: Paul's Personal Pentecost

Just as Paul was an exception to the apostolic order, there was an exception made as to his experience of the Holy Spirit's empowerment as an Apostle. Just as his calling was different from the other Apostles, so his anointing in conjunction with that vocation was different as well. The other Apostles received this power in Acts chapter two as a group. Paul received his anointing of apostolic power under much different circumstances.

As we look at this event in Paul's life, let us begin by remembering those circumstances. Saul of Tarsus is first mentioned in Acts 8:1, affirming and endorsing the death of Stephan. He was "Saul the Enforcer" then, persecuting the church of Jesus Christ. Acts chapter nine records that on his way to Damascus, Paul encountered the Lord Jesus Christ and was blinded. Taken into the city by his associates, Paul waited for what came next.

The Lord Jesus appeared in a vision to a disciple named Ananias. We are not told that there was anything particularly significant about Ananias. He was not an Apostle. He was not a church leader to our knowledge. There are certain traditions associated with him, but how reliable those are is anyone's guess.

The fact is, we are not supposed to be impressed with Ananias' credentials. The Lord could have arranged for an Apostle to be in Damascus. He could have arranged for Philip to be "teleported" there as he did earlier (Acts 8:39), but he chose Ananias to be the one to restore Paul's sight, impart the filling of the Holy Spirit and baptize Paul.

From our understanding, Ananias was an ordinary believer referred to in the text simply as a "disciple". (Acts 9:10) We are not told much about him. Paul, referring to him later, tells us that Ananias was "a devout man according to the law, having a good report of all the Jews which dwelt *there*" (Acts 22:12).

The Lord Jesus told Ananias to go to Saul and place His hands upon him. The placement of the hands directly by the command of the Lord was to accomplish two tasks. One was to bring sight to Saul's blinded eyes. The other was for him to be filled with the Holy Spirit. Note the text:

> "And Ananias went his way, and entered into the house; and putting his hands on him said, Brother Saul, the Lord, even Jesus, that appeared unto thee in the way as thou camest, hath sent me, that thou mightest receive thy sight, and be filled with the Holy Ghost. And immediately there fell from his eyes as it had been scales: and he received sight forthwith, and arose, and was baptized." (Act 9:17-18)

Ananias then drops out of the picture, but Paul's role as God's preacher was off and running. Empowered with the Spirit, one would have expected an immediate conference with the other Apostles introducing him as their new colleague, but no. God had other plans for Paul that were not to be connected with the ideas and influence of the others. Paul details what happened next in Galatians:

> "But when it pleased God, who separated me from my mother's womb, and called me by his grace, To reveal his Son in me, that I might preach him

among the heathen; immediately I conferred not with flesh and blood: Neither went I up to Jerusalem to them which were apostles before me; but I went into Arabia, and returned again unto Damascus. Then after three years I went up to Jerusalem to see Peter, and abode with him fifteen days. But other of the apostles saw I none, save James the Lord's brother. Now the things which I write unto you, behold, before God, I lie not. Afterwards I came into the regions of Syria and Cilicia; And was unknown by face unto the churches of Judaea which were in Christ: But they had heard only, That he which persecuted us in times past now preacheth the faith which once he destroyed. And they glorified God in me." (Galatians 1:15-24)

Paul relates in this passage that God sent him into obscurity. He makes a point of saying that "...immediately I conferred not with flesh and blood: Neither went I up to Jerusalem to them which were apostles before me..." (Galatians 1:16 b-17a).

What was happening to Paul in Arabia? Why does he make a point of saying that he did not meet with even one Apostle for the first three years after his conversion? Then he makes a point of saying that even when he met one, it was only for 15 days! This writer believes that the purpose of all this was to establish the independent and unique nature of his Apostleship -- that Paul was not subservient or inferior to the original Twelve. Paul clearly tells the Corinthians that he was not inferior to the other Apostles.

> "For I suppose I was not a whit behind the very chiefest apostles." (II Corinthians 11:5)

He then tells them that his knowledge of the things of God was not in any way inferior to the other Apostles:

> "But though I be rude in speech, yet not in knowledge;" (II Corinthians 11:6)

We know that at some point in this time frame in Arabia he was given an "abundance of ... revelations" (II Corinthians 12:7), so much so that the Lord had to give him a physical ailment to keep him humble and, therefore, useful.

The point of all this is that Paul's calling was to be wholly unconnected with the other Apostles. That is the way the Lord Jesus custom-designed his ministry. Because he became an Apostle as one "born out of due time", a commission from the other Apostles would seem to necessitate that his office was given from them or created by them. Therefore, Paul begins the letter to the Galatians by stating unequivocally:

> "Paul, an apostle, (not of men, neither by man, but by Jesus Christ, and God the Father, who raised him from the dead;)" (Galatians 1:1)

It is therefore not surprising that Paul was an exception to the general rule of the empowerment by the laying on of the Apostles' hands. Paul received his "personal Pentecost" under special circumstances.

There was no question in Paul's mind that the Lord Jesus Christ had met him on the Damascus road and called him to preach. Paul was absolutely certain as to his Apostleship being on the same level as the other Apostles. What one writer called "Paul's vocational self-consciousness" was never at question in his own mind.[1] However, it was often at issue in the minds of others as has been already demonstrated. Paul faced this challenge to his Apostleship many times as we have already witnessed in his defense of it in Corinth.

He also alludes to this issue in the book of Galatians. The churches Paul had established in Gaul had been influenced by "Christian" Jewish teachers who maintained that salvation came, at least in part, by law-keeping. The same teachers apparently had questioned Paul's apostolic authority. The strategy was to bring disrepute upon the messenger and then subvert the message. They were saying that the Gospel that Paul preached was of his own concoction. In essence, they were saying that Paul was a freelance religionist who had no connection to the other Apostles and had introduced a false gospel.

The beginning salvo of the epistle to the Galatians is to establish that his Apostleship was not of human origin. It was.*"...not of men"*. It did not come from the consensus, opinions or the authority of men. No committee was formed to examine his credentials or suitability for the job. Neither was it "of man." It did not come from an

---

[1] Hawthorne, G. F., Martin, R. P., & Reid, D. G. 1993. Dictionary of Paul and his letters. InterVarsity Press: Downers Grove, Ill. P. 617

individual's idea. It was not something that Paul just decided on his own. His Apostleship came from "Jesus Christ and God the Father who raised him from the dead" (Galatians 1:1). Paul maintains that just as his Apostleship was separate from any man, the Gospel that he preached was not of human origin as well.

> "But I certify you, brethren, that the gospel which was preached of me is not after man. For I neither received it of man, neither was I taught it, but by the revelation of Jesus Christ." (Galatians 1:11-12)

He then makes the point that he was independent of any man's teaching including the other Apostles. Paul, in the rest of chapter one and all of chapter two, details his activities since his conversion. He makes a point of saying that he is not self-made. Neither was he subservient to or inferior to other church leaders or the Apostles.

In fact, he maintains that he was not swayed or impressed with the reputation or influence of others at a meeting with the Apostles in Jerusalem. As one reads the narrative, one can see the independence and equality of calling that Paul is maintaining. He even confronted the Apostle Peter for his inconsistent behavior in reference to the Gospel. (Galatians 2:11) So much for the supposed Petrine supremacy of the church!

> "To whom we gave place by subjection, no, not for an hour; that the truth of the gospel might continue with you. But of these who seemed to be somewhat, (whatsoever they were, it maketh no matter to me:

God accepteth no man's person:) for they who seemed to be somewhat in conference added nothing to me:
But contrariwise, when they saw that the gospel of the uncircumcision was committed unto me, as the gospel of the circumcision was unto Peter; (For he that wrought effectually in Peter to the apostleship of the circumcision, the same was mighty in me toward the Gentiles:) And when James, Cephas, and John, who seemed to be pillars, perceived the grace that was given unto me, they gave to me and Barnabas the right hands of fellowship; that we should go unto the heathen, and they unto the circumcision. Only they would that we should remember the poor; the same which I also was forward to do. But when Peter was come to Antioch, I withstood him to the face, because he was to be blamed. For before that certain came from James, he did eat with the Gentiles: but when they were come, he withdrew and separated himself, fearing them which were of the circumcision. And the other Jews dissembled likewise with him; insomuch that Barnabas also was carried away with their dissimulation. But when I saw that they walked not uprightly according to the truth of the gospel, I said unto Peter before them all, If thou, being a Jew, livest after the manner of Gentiles, and not as do the Jews, why compellest thou the Gentiles to live as do the Jews?"
(Galatians 2:5-14)

In the above narrative Paul is pointing out several things:

-His message was divine, not earthly
(Galatians1:11-12)

-His calling was divine, not of men or of himself.
(Galatians 1:1,12)

-His ministry was unaffected and independent of other church leaders.
(Galatians 2:5-6)

-His ministry was endorsed by the other Apostles.
(Galatians 2:7-9)

-He confronted the error of another Apostle – Peter.
(Galatians 2:11-21)

The point being made is that his ministry was separate and distinct from the other Apostles. As such, his commission and empowerment was as well.

Exception #2: The Gentile Pentecost

Modern believers forget the unique "Jewishness" of Christianity, yet what we term "Christianity" started among Jews. The only Christians in that initial time frame were Jews. To those early believers there was no sense that following Jesus made them adherents to a different religion than the Judaism with which they were familiar. To them, they had accepted the Jewish Messiah who had died for and risen from the dead for His people. They had no sense of *ceasing* to be Jewish. They had no thought of leaving their synagogues or of refusing to participate in the feasts or practices at the temple. They certainly had no sense that God might reach out to non-Jews.

Think of it! The majority of recorded biblical history recorded from Genesis through Acts chapter eight are primarily dealing with one race of people -- Jews! There are exceptions but the primary attention is on God's people Israel. Jesus Christ was a Jew. He chose Twelve Jewish men to be His Apostles. The initial baptism of the Spirit in Acts two happened to twelve Jewish men who in turn bestowed it only to Jewish men and women.

The first suggestion that something new was afoot was when Philip went down to Samaria (Acts eight). To many Jews, the Samaritans were a step in between them and Gentiles. They were *quasi-Jews* so to speak. Most Jews considered the Samaritans to be unclean and "good Jews" would not have anything to do with them. When the woman at the well said to Jesus that the "…Jews have no dealings with the Samaritans" (John 4:9), it was no flippant statement. This is why she considered it so remarkable that Jesus spoke with her.

According to the Jews, the Samaritans were descendants from transplanted Assyrian colonists who adopted the faith of the Jews in the north of Israel. The Samaritans were considered by the Jews of Judah to be "Jewish-*ish*" but not Jews and therefore not of the nation. The Samaritans believed that they maintained the pristine faith of the Pentateuch and that the Jews had corrupted the faith. For the Samaritan, being an Israelite was more religious than racial. Josephus, the Jewish historian records that there was a degree of "Jewishness" to

Samaritan religious customs.[2] Perhaps that is why there was more acceptance of them, than of Gentiles in general.

Acts chapter eight records that Philip went down to Samaria to preach Jesus Christ and the Samaritans responded in faith. When word reached The Twelve that the Samaritans had believed they sent two Apostles down to investigate. Peter and John, realizing that these Samaritans had believed and, no doubt remembering the Lord's ministry to them, were not hesitant to lay hands upon them and give them the baptism of the Holy Spirit.

> "Now when the apostles which were at Jerusalem heard that Samaria had received the word of God, they sent unto them Peter and John: Who, when they were come down, prayed for them, that they might receive the Holy Ghost: (For as yet he was fallen upon none of them: only they were baptized in the name of the Lord Jesus.) Then laid they their hands on them, and they received the Holy Ghost." (Acts 8:14 - 17)

Though the Samaritans were accepted as believers, out and out Gentiles were not going to be accepted so readily by the Apostles and the early Jewish church. This would be a major hurdle to them and the turmoil and turning point is documented in chapters ten and eleven of the book of Acts.

"Non-Jews were looked upon with suspicion and were not associated with by Jews. Intermarriage between Jews

---

[2]Green, Joel 1992 Dictionary of Jesus and the Gospels, InterVarsity Press: Downers Grove, Ill. P 72

and Gentiles was forbidden. In Jesus' day, one was considered unclean if he touched a Gentile. The "hands-off" policy extended even after the door of salvation was opened to the Gentiles." [3]

The gist of Acts chapter ten is that Peter was sent a vision of animals forbidden as food by Jewish law and commanded to eat them. As a devout Jew, he refused, considering them unclean. God rebuked him and told him to stop calling what God had cleansed unclean. Cornelius, a Roman, had sent servants to bring Peter to him. Peter, connecting the lesson of his vision to the request of this Gentile to come, got the message. When Peter arrived at Cornelius' house

> "....he said unto them, Ye know how that it is an unlawful thing for a man that is a Jew to keep company, or come unto one of another nation; but God hath showed me that I should not call any man common or unclean."(Acts 10:28)

Even then it did not occur to Peter that God wanted him to proclaim the gospel to Gentiles. He simply asked this Roman why he had asked him to come. (verse 29)

Cornelius then explains how God had prompted him to summon Peter to hear something special. (Acts 10:30-33) A profound truth dawns upon Peter concerning what God was communicating to him.

> "Then Peter opened his mouth, and said, Of a truth I perceive that God is no respecter of persons:

---

3 Gill, John *John Gill's Exposition of the Entire Bible* Notes on Acts 10:15,28,34

> But in every nation he that feareth him, and
> worketh righteousness, is accepted with him."
> (Acts 10: 34-35)

Peter then communicates the gospel message of peace with God through Jesus Christ who was slain on a tree, arisen from the dead and personally witnessed to be alive by the Apostles (Acts 10: 39-43). As Peter closes his message to them, he says:

> "....To him give all the prophets witness, that
> through his name whosoever believeth in him
> shall receive remission of sins. " (Acts 10:43)

Then something totally unexpected happened. As Peter shared this wonderful news of the living Christ and forgiveness in Him, a manifestation of the Holy Spirit paralleling what happened to the Apostles at Pentecost took place. Only this time, the Holy Spirit was resting upon Gentiles! This was a stunning development and very different from what had happened in Samaria! Peter, who possessed the ability to impart the baptism of the Holy Spirit and who did so in Samaria, stood and watched God do the unthinkable -- come upon Gentiles in power as He had come upon Jewish believers in Christ!

The Jewish believers that had accompanied Peter were astonished at what had happened ..."because that on the Gentiles also was poured out the gift of the Holy Ghost" (verse 45), Peter asks his colleagues whether there can be any objections to these Gentiles following in believer's baptism when it was obvious that God had accepted them.

Apparently there were no objections in that business meeting! (Verse 47-48)

One would think that the case of God's acceptance of the Gentiles would be closed among their Jewish brethren. Not so! When Peter returned to Jerusalem there was a bit of an upset. The news had traveled quickly that the Gentiles had received the gospel. Peter had remained a few days with these Gentiles and that, in itself, caused a stir:

> "And when Peter was come up to Jerusalem, they
> that were of the circumcision contended with him,
> Saying, Thou wentest in to men uncircumcised, and
> didst eat with them." (Act 11:2-3)

Peter gave a detailed explanation of what had happened. The majority of the believers in Jerusalem were convinced that God had extended salvation to the Gentiles. The incontrovertible proof was this impartation of the Spirit to the Gentiles.

> "And as I began to speak, the Holy Ghost fell on
> them, as on us at the beginning. Then remembered
> I the word of the Lord, how that he said, John indeed
> baptized with water; but ye shall be baptized with the
> Holy Ghost. Forasmuch then as **God gave them
> the like gift** as he did unto us, who believed on the
> Lord Jesus Christ; what was I, that I could withstand
> God? When they heard these things, they held
> their peace, and glorified God, saying, Then hath
> God also to the Gentiles granted repentance unto
> life." (Acts 11:15-18)

Peter and the others present with those Gentiles had their doubts dispelled about what God wanted in reference to them by the "Gentile Pentecost." The "gift" that God had given them was all the proof that was needed to show that God was now including Gentiles in His redemptive plan. His doing so was an exceptional occurrence for an exceptional purpose.

Appendix 2

The Many Uses of the Word "Baptize"

"Baptizo" is Explained

There was a poem that I came across many years ago. It was written back in the 1800's by Eugene Field. It a poem about a little boy that loved the food at the various church picnics. He named off several denominations and how the food compared from one picnic to another. For what its worth, his conclusion was that the Presbyterians had the best food. However, here are the lines of this poem that have stuck in my head all these many years:

> "One year I jined the Baptists,
>   an' goodness! how it rained!
> (But grampa says that that's the way
>   "baptizo" is explained.)" [1]

Well, grandpa's understanding of "baptizo", the Greek word from which the English word "baptism" is transliterated, needed some further elaboration, if you ask me. Indeed, an understanding of the word "baptizo" is one of the "watershed" issues (pun intended) dividing denominations and on which doctrines have been founded.

It is interesting to this author that the Greek word "baptizo" is, to his knowledge, the only word in the Bible that is *transliterated* rather than translated. The distinction between a transliterated word and a translated

---
[1] Picnic Time by Eugene Field (1850-1895) PoemHunter.Com

word is profound. To transliterate a word is to take a word from one language and turn it into a similar sounding word in another language. A *translated* word from one language to another is to convey the *meaning* of that word.

The word "baptize" is such a transliterated word. It was not translated as to its meaning but transliterated into an English word. Had it been translated, much of the confusion and division today between denominations may have been avoided. I say, *much* could be avoided but certainly not all. For explaining "baptizo" is largely dependent on the context of the passage in which it is used. Most folks, when thinking of the word "baptize", reflexively think about water baptism. However, often the word is used and is not connected with water at all!

Dive! Dive!

The Greek word "baptizo" can have a variety of meanings depending on the context of a passage. It can mean to dip, to immerse, or to submerge. Sometimes it can mean to cleanse by submerging. It is used in connection with washing or to making clean with water, i.e. bathing. It can sometimes mean to overwhelm as in being overcome by overwhelming enemy numbers. It also is used with the idea of incorporating or initiating into or unto something or someone. The general idea is one of submersing. Sometimes, however, the sense of its meaning can only be determined by the context in which it is used.

There are essentially three senses in which the concept of baptism is employed in Scripture.

Identification

Identification or association is connected with the word baptize. It is used in this sense referring to the Israelites being *"baptized unto Moses"* when God's people passed through God's Shekinah glory and experienced the deliverance in following him through the Red Sea.

> "Moreover, brethren, I would not that ye should be ignorant, how that all our fathers were under the cloud, and all passed through the sea; And were all **baptized unto Moses** in the cloud and in the sea;" (I Corinthians 10:1-2)

This usage of the word "baptism" had nothing to do with water baptism. The point that the writer is making is that the Israelites were *identified* with the promises of God and His deliverance through Moses. They were *"baptized unto Moses"*. This baptism's "elements" were not water but were God's glory -- the cloud and His deliverance through the sea. The associative aspects of this baptism were God's promises and, by extension, His covenant with Moses.

The idea of identification and association is further seen in the baptism of John the Baptist. Paul states that the meaning of John's baptism was clear:

> "And it came to pass, that, while Apollos was at Corinth, Paul having passed through the upper

coasts came to Ephesus: and finding certain disciples, He said unto them, Have ye received the Holy Ghost since ye believed? And they said unto him, We have not so much as heard whether there be any Holy Ghost. And he said unto them, Unto what then were ye baptized? And they said, Unto John's baptism. Then said Paul, John verily baptized with the baptism of repentance, saying unto the people, that they should believe on him which should come after him, that is, on Christ Jesus." (Acts 19:1-4)

John's baptism identified those who participated in it with a repentant heart and an expectant faith in the appearance of the Messiah. That was its meaning.

Incorporation

There is also a usage of the word "baptizo" that means to submerse into. It is this usage that refers to the placement into the organic presence of Christ in conjunction with regeneration. The Bible refers to this as being *"baptized into Christ."* This is the usage of the word in Galatians.

> "For as many of you as have been baptized into Christ have put on Christ." (Galatians 3:27)

The Bible is also clear that the means of this *placing into* is accomplished through the Holy Spirit, not water. The idea is of "placement into" in regard to being incorporated into the body of Christ through the Holy Spirit. In 1 Corinthians we read:

> "For by one Spirit are we all baptized into one body, whether we be Jews or Gentiles, whether we be bond or free; and have been all made to drink into one Spirit." (I Corinthians 12:13)

The usage of the word *baptize* in this context carries with it the idea of placement or submersing into of both Jews and Gentiles into one body. This unity of Jew and Gentile was accomplished by the Holy Spirit and does not refer to water baptism at all. This *placement* is also spoken of in Romans 6:1-6 in reference to being incorporated into the person of Christ. There is a vicarious participation in the death of Jesus Christ accomplished through this spiritual baptism.

> "Know ye not, that so many of us as were baptized into Jesus Christ were baptized into his death?" (Romans 6:3)

In the baptism of incorporation, the believer is not baptized *with* the Holy Spirit or *in* the Holy Spirit but *by* the Holy Spirit. The Holy Spirit is the agent who does the baptizing into the body of Christ. He is the One Who places the believer in Christ. In this baptism, the Lord Jesus is the One into Whom the believer is being immersed and the Holy Spirit is the One doing the immersing.

Empowerment

The baptism of empowerment is a supernatural acting of the presence of God in divine empowerment. It is what the Lord Jesus Christ promised His Apostles and what was given to them and others in the early church. This was the baptism that empowered the Apostles and was manifested in the "Gentile Pentecost". (See Appendix 1). The idea here is one of engulfing or encompassing the individual in the power of the Holy Spirit. The promise is reiterated in several places.

> "I indeed have baptized you with water: but he shall baptize you with the Holy Ghost." (Mark 1:8)

> "And, being assembled together with them, commanded them that they should not depart from Jerusalem, but wait for the promise of the Father, which, saith he, ye have heard of me. For John truly baptized with water; but ye shall be baptized with the Holy Ghost not many days hence." (Acts 1:4-5)

It is what the Lord promised in Luke 24.

> "And, behold, I send the promise of my Father upon you: but tarry ye in the city of Jerusalem, until ye be endued with power from on high." (Luke 24:49)

It is evident that this baptism refers to divine empowerment in the following passage in the Gentile Pentecost. (See Appendix 1.)

> "And as I began to speak, the Holy Ghost fell on them, as on us at the beginning. Then remembered I the word of the Lord, how that

he said, John indeed baptized with water;
but ye shall be baptized with the Holy Ghost."
(Acts 11:15-16)

The baptism of empowerment was not connected with water and was by or through the ministry of the Apostles As such, it is not for today.

Water Baptism

Water baptism was not strictly a Christian practice. Jews, such as the Essenes, practiced water baptism. John the Baptist practiced baptism for those who were of a repentant heart. It is obvious that this water baptism is total immersion (the meaning of the word *baptizo*) in water. There would be no need to *go down into the water* as the Scripture states if it was not immersion.

> "And there went out unto him all the land of Judaea, and they of Jerusalem, and were all baptized of him **in the river** of Jordan, confessing their sins." (Mark 1:5)

> "And Jesus, when he was baptized, went up straightway **out of the water**: and, lo, the heavens were opened unto him, and he saw the Spirit of God descending like a dove, and lighting upon him:" (Matthew 3:16)

> "And he commanded the chariot to stand still: and **they went down both into the water,** both Philip and the eunuch; and he baptized him." (Acts 8:38)

Water baptism carried with it the symbolism of cleansing or washing. While water baptism has no *actual* ability to cleanse us from sin, Peter elaborates that baptism cleanses by showing the figure, or symbolism of it. In his first epistle, chapter three, Peter speaks of the Noahic world and how Noah and his family were "saved" by water.

> "Which sometime were disobedient, when once the longsuffering of God waited in the days of Noah, while the ark was a preparing, wherein few, that is, eight souls were saved by water. The like figure whereunto even baptism doth also now save us (not the putting away of the filth of the flesh, but the answer of a good conscience toward *God*,) **by the resurrection of Jesus Christ...**" (I Peter 3:20-21)

In the case of Noah and his family being saved through the flood judgment, it was not the water that did the saving. The *ark* was the means of saving those folks via the water. In like figure, Peter says, baptism saves us, not by any actual cleansing of or from fleshly sinful actions but by pointing us toward the resurrected Christ Who shed His blood on the cross. Baptism, Peter says, does not put away *"the filth of the flesh"*. It has no actual saving cleansing power. The resurrected Lord Jesus Christ does the saving.

When a person is baptized unto Christ they are declaring that they have participated in the cleansing that comes through faith in His name. Their conscience toward God is secure in that they have obeyed God and identified with the Savior. Therefore, it is not the act of baptism that saves, it is the Person Jesus Christ Who saves through repentance and faith in His work on the cross and resurrection from the dead. Baptism in the name of Jesus was synonymous with a confession of faith in His saving work.

Water baptism does not save, but saved folks will be baptized and have the assurance of a good conscience toward God because of it. That is what Peter was meaning when he claims that *baptism doth save us.* It is in that understanding that other passages that speak of water baptism must be understood (i.e., Mark 16:16; Acts 2:38; Acts 22: 16).

(For further discussion of water baptism and salvation, see Appendix 3.: Does Water Baptism save?)

So the transliterated term "baptize" or "baptism" is used in at least four different senses in the Scripture. Depending on the context the word may be understood as water baptism, Spirit empowerment, incorporation into or identification with. Only the context determines how this transliterated, rather than translated, word must be understood.

Frank I. Snyder

Appendix 3

Does Water Baptism Save?

Are there passages in the Scripture that seem to connect cleansing from sin and forgiveness with water baptism? Honesty dictates that there are some places in the Bible that seem to bear this out such as these passages:

> "He that believeth and is baptized shall be saved; but he that believeth not shall be damned." (Mark 16:16)

> "Then Peter said unto them, Repent, and be baptized every one of you in the name of Jesus Christ for the remission of sins, and ye shall receive the gift of the Holy Ghost." (Acts 2:38)

> "And now why tarriest thou? arise, and be baptized, and wash away thy sins, calling on the name of the Lord." (Acts 22:16)

The above passages are the three main passages of Scripture that those who believe baptism is essential to salvation would cite to prove their case. Certainly, taken by themselves without any other passage of Scripture being consulted, the case would be very strong that lack of baptism would lead one to be eternally condemned, that sins would not be remitted, and that water baptism washes away sins.

However, there are legitimate reasons to believe that, though baptism is important, it is ancillary to salvation and not actually *part* of being saved. What reasons are these?

The teaching that baptism cleanses away sin conflicts with the plain statements in Scripture to the efficacy of the blood of Christ as the salvific (saving) means of cleansing and forgiveness.

The Scripture is clear that *"...* **the blood of Jesus Christ his Son cleanseth us** from all sin" (1 John 1:7).

> "Being justified freely by his grace through the redemption that is in Christ Jesus: Whom God hath set forth to be a propitiation **through faith in his blood**, to declare his righteousness **for the remission of sins** that are past, through the forbearance of God;" (Rom 3:24-25)
>
> "Much more then, **being now justified by his blood, we shall be saved from wrath** through him." (Romans 5:9)
>
> "In whom **we have redemption through his blood, the forgiveness of sins**, according to the riches of his grace;" (Ephesians 1:7)
>
> "In whom **we have redemption through his blood, even the forgiveness of sins**:" (Colossians 1:14)

Even the memorial of the Lord's supper gives the symbol in the cup as *representing* the blood that Christ shed on the cross.

> "And he took the cup, and gave thanks, and gave it to them, saying, Drink ye all of it; For **this is my blood** of the new testament, **which is shed for many for the remission of sins**." (Matthew 26:27-28)

Lest anyone think that the literal contents of the cup is what saves (i.e. the ingested wine), Colossians 1:20 clearly points out that He, Jesus, *"made peace through the blood of his cross..."*.

So if water baptism remits, washes, forgives, and cleanses sin, then there is a very clear contradiction in Scripture as to the *agent* of cleansing. If water contributes to the cleansing, then the efficacy of the blood of Christ is diluted in some way.

The teaching that baptism cleanses away sin conflicts with the Bible's emphasis that it is one's faith and not baptism in water that God counts for righteousness.

Though there is clearly a connection with a professed willingness to be baptized and the presence of genuine faith, the Bible is clear that salvation results only through repentant faith in the redemptive sacrifice of Christ on the cross and His resurrection. If Scripture teaches the necessity of baptism, it would seem to be that God Himself was adding a work to the salvation that is "not of works".

> "For by grace are ye saved through **faith**; and that not of yourselves: it is the gift of God:

Not of works, lest any man should boast. "
(Ephesians 2:8-9)

The same Peter who said in Acts 2:38 "Repent, and be baptized every one of you in the name of Jesus Christ for the remission of sins, and ye shall receive the gift of the Holy Ghost", later says in Acts ten at the "Gentile Pentecost" that "whosoever **believeth** in him shall receive remission of sins" (Acts 10:43). Peter, in speaking to the Gentiles just preceding the "Gentile Pentecost", does not mention water baptism as being part of the saving process. He tells those believers that believing in the person and work of Jesus Christ results in remission of sins.

After the Gentiles had believed, God validated their acceptance with Him through sending a baptism of the Holy Spirit similar to what had happened to the Apostles in Acts two. Note Acts 10:44:

"While Peter yet spake these words, the Holy
Ghost fell on all them which heard the word. "

The reader will note the sequence of events. Peter preached and the Gentiles responded in faith. *Before* they were baptized, God validated His acceptance of them through Holy Spirit baptism. Only then did Peter authorize them to be baptized in water (Acts 10: 47). If when the Gentile believers responded in faith, God bestowed this baptism of the Spirit, they had to have been forgiven and cleansed even though they had not yet been baptized in water. If water baptism was essential to salvation, then we would be witnessing Gentile believers that had been empowered by the Holy Spirit but were not yet cleansed of their sin (if baptism literally washes away sin).

It may be argued that these Gentiles were not yet believers, yet Peter, at the Jerusalem council (Acts 15), elaborates on exactly what happened that day.

> "Men and brethren, ye know how that a good while ago God made choice among us, that the Gentiles by my mouth should hear the word of the gospel, and believe. And God, which knoweth the hearts, bare them witness, giving them the Holy Ghost, even as he did unto us; And put no difference between us and them, **purifying their hearts by faith**." (Acts 15:7-9)

Note that Peter says that the Gentiles heard the word of the Gospel and believed. Peter states that the God who looked into their hearts bore witness to their faith by giving them the gift of the Spirit. Peter said that God purified their hearts when they placed their faith in Christ. The reader will remember that these believers' water baptism did not occur until *after* all of this had taken place. It is clear that these Gentiles had believed the Gospel and were cleansed (purified) by faith *before* they were baptized in water.

Certainly, that order is consistent with the preponderance of Scripture that salvation comes by placing one's faith in the Person and finished work of Christ. Even a brief perusal of the Scriptural evidence makes it clear that believing brings salvation.

"Be it known unto you therefore, men and brethren, that through this man is preached unto you **the forgiveness of sins: And by him all that believe are justified from all things**, from which ye could not be justified by the law of Moses." (Act 13:38-39)

"Therefore **we conclude that a man is justified by faith** without the deeds of the law." (Romans 3:28)

"Therefore **being justified by faith, we have peace with God through our Lord Jesus Christ: By whom also we have access by faith into this grace** wherein we stand, and rejoice in hope of the glory of God." (Romans 5:1-2)

"Knowing that **a man is not justified by the works of the law, but by the faith of Jesus Christ, even we have believed in Jesus Christ, that we might be justified by the faith of Christ**, and not by the works of the law: for by the works of the law shall no flesh be justified." (Galatians 2:16)

"But that no man is justified by the law in the sight of God, it is evident: for, **The just shall live by faith**." (Galatians 3:11)

"But the scripture hath concluded all under sin, that **the promise by faith of Jesus Christ might**

be given to them that believe. But before faith came, we were kept under the law, shut up unto the faith which should afterwards be revealed. Wherefore the law was our schoolmaster to bring us unto Christ, **that we might be justified by faith**." (Galatians 3:22-24)

"**For by grace are ye saved through faith**; and that not of yourselves: it is the gift of God: Not of works, lest any man should boast." (Ephesians 2:8-9)

Three Problematic Passages

So, given the historical narrative in the book of Acts and the above testimony in Scripture as to salvation being "sola fide" (only by faith), how should we understand water baptism and its connection, if any, to salvation? Specifically, how are we to understand the aforementioned passages in the Scripture which seem to testify that water baptism has, in some sense, a cleansing /saving effect on the sinner. Let us look at these again.

"He that believeth and is baptized shall be saved; but he that believeth not shall be damned." (Mark 16:16)

The reader will note that is those that *believe not* that are condemned (damned). Refusing to exercise faith in Christ has the result of condemnation, not lack of baptism. The question is: What is essential? The baptism of a believer is assumed but it is the believing that is essential. Perhaps an illustration would be helpful.

If you were to travel from New Jersey to New York City across the Hudson River via the ferry, I could accurately say, "Whoever sits on the ferry in New Jersey will arrive in New York." Sitting down is assumed but in reality is incidental to arriving in New York. Having ridden that ferry, the writer can testify that most people do, indeed, sit during that short jaunt. In fact, I think that the operator would *prefer* that riders sit down, but the fact is that some stand. Either way, arriving in New York is not dependent on whether one sits, stands, stoops, crouches, cowers or reclines. It is dependent upon being on board. Getting on board is crucial to getting to New York.

Believing is the crucial aspect. *Not believing* results in condemnation. John 3:18 says:

> "He that **believeth on him** is **not condemned**: but he that believeth not is condemned already, because he hath not believed in the name of the only begotten Son of God."

Baptism is a natural normal result of believing, but it *is* distinct from believing. Is baptism important? Yes. Is it vital to getting saving acceptance with God? No.

The ferry analogy above breaks down, of course, when one compares the importance of baptism versus how unimportant sitting or standing on a ferry to New York is. Still, the issue is one of *essentiality*. Baptism of believers is assumed for a believer, but not a requirement for salvation!

But what about Acts 2:38?

> "Then Peter said unto them, Repent, and be baptized every one of you in the name of Jesus Christ for the remission of sins, and ye shall receive the gift of the Holy Ghost."

Again, the importance of baptism is assumed. The key word and phrase, however, in this passage are the words "Repent" and "in the name of Jesus Christ for the remission of sins."

The use of the word repent is, in most cases, synonymous with believing. The Scripture attests that remission of sins happens upon both repentance *and* belief indicating they are one and the same event. Jesus, in His post-resurrection appearance to the disciples on the road to Emmaus, tells the disciples that "repentance and remission of sins should be preached in his name...." (Luke 24:47)

Repentance was certainly part of the message of the early church.

> "The God of our fathers raised up Jesus, whom ye slew and hanged on a tree. Him hath God exalted with his right hand to be a Prince and a Savior, **for to give repentance to Israel, and forgiveness of sins.**" (Act 5:30 - 31)

However, from the explanation that Peter gave to the Jerusalem Council regarding the inclusion of the

Gentiles, it is evident that repentance and faith are synonymous terms. In the following verses, note the phrase "believed on the Lord Jesus Christ" and note the conclusion of the Council that God had granted "the Gentiles repentance unto life".

> "Forasmuch then as God gave them the like gift as he did unto us, **who believed on the Lord Jesus Christ**; what was I, that I could withstand God? When they heard these things, they held their peace, and glorified God, saying, Then hath God also to the **Gentiles granted repentance unto life.**" (Act 11:17-18)

Paul's ministry to the Gentiles was one of testifying "repentance toward God, and faith toward our Lord Jesus Christ." (Act 20:21)

So repenting and believing are used almost interchangeably in Scripture. The result of repentance and believing was remission of sins. Again, repentance and believing are used interchangeably and result in forgiveness, remission of sin, etc. Peter certainly connected the words *believe* with *repent* and *remission* with *justification*.

> "Repent ye therefore, and be converted, that your sins may be blotted out, when the times of refreshing shall come from the presence of the Lord;" (Act 3:19)

> "Be it known unto you therefore, men and brethren, that through this man is preached unto

you **the forgiveness of sins**: And by him **all that believe are justified** from all things, from which ye could not be justified by the law of Moses." (Act 13:38-39)

So it is clear that repenting and believing are linked in reference to remission of sins. Thus when Peter uses the word "Repent!" in Acts 2:38, he is saying to these Jewish people gathered there – "Believe!" We have already cited numerous passages of Scripture proving that forgiveness justification, remission of sins, etc., happens by *believing* on Christ. (Acts 13:38 -39; Rom 3:28 ; Rom 5:1 -2; Gal 2:16 ; Gal 3:11, 22-24; Eph 2:8-9)

The first part of Acts 2:38 is "repent" meaning "believe". Then comes the next phrase "and be baptized" indicating the importance of baptism, but not necessarily its essentiality to salvation. The essential aspect of this verse is the phrase "in the name of Jesus Christ for the remission of sins." Remission of sins happens when a person believes in the name of Jesus Christ! To believe on the name means to believe on the person. Note the following:

> "But these are written, that ye might believe that Jesus is the Christ, the Son of God; and that believing ye might have life **through his name**" (John 20:31)

> "And such were some of you: but ye are **washed**, but ye are **sanctified**, but ye are **justified in the name of the Lord Jesus**, and by the Spirit of our God." (I Corinthians 6:11)

> "I write unto you, little children, because **your sins are forgiven you for his name's sake.**" (I John 2:12)

Peter commands them to repent (believe) in the name of Jesus Christ for the remission of sins. Yes, baptism is interjected in the verse because it is assumed that those who believe on Christ will identify with Him in baptism, but it is the believing on the name of Jesus Christ that saves! Peter plainly declares this truth later in Acts.

> "To him give all the prophets witness, that **through his name** whosoever believeth in him shall receive remission of sins." (Acts 10:43)

Remember the context of that verse? Gentiles heard the gospel of Christ and believed, followed by God bearing witness of their conversion to Christ through the gift of the Holy Sprit (Acts 10:44). Peter, later recounting the same event, states that their hearts had been purified by faith before they had been baptized (Act 15:8-9). Baptism was commanded after they believed, received remission of sins, were accepted by God, born witness to as accepted and purified by Him. (Acts 10:47-48)

Thus, the conclusion of this writer based upon the testimony of the one through whom the Holy Spirit spoke (Peter) is that water baptism is corollary to but not ancillary to salvation. In other words, it is the natural result of believing but it is not essential to salvation.

The final verse in question is Ananias' words to Paul the Apostle in Acts chapter 22.

> "And now why tarriest thou? arise, and be baptized, and wash away thy sins, calling on the name of the Lord." (Acts 22:16)

When Paul was told by Ananias to arise and be baptized and wash his sins away, was Ananias attributing a cleansing effect to water baptism or was he attaching the remission of sins to Paul's "calling upon the name of the Lord"? What has calling on the name of the Lord have to do with salvation?

Perhaps looking at statements from the Apostle Paul himself would add clarity, especially since he was the one admonished by Ananias to wash away his sins.

We have already cited several passages indicating that Paul nowhere indicates that anything but the blood of Christ cleanses from sin. (Romans 3:24-25; 5:9; Ephesians 1:7; Colossians 1:14) Further, we have seen that believing on the name of the Lord is equivalent to trusting in the Lord Himself for salvation. (John 20:31; I Corinthians 6:11; I John 2:12).

Understanding Acts 22:16 is conditioned upon understanding that "calling on the name of the Lord" is equivalent to believing. Paul himself indicates this in his statements recorded in Romans ten. Note what Romans says about how righteousness is achieved and the connection with "calling upon the name of the Lord." Note that there is no mention of water baptism at all. What is testified with the mouth is a reflection of the heart.

> "That if thou shalt confess with thy mouth the
> Lord Jesus, and shalt believe in thine heart that
> God hath raised him from the dead, thou shalt be
> saved. For with the heart man believeth unto
> righteousness; and with the mouth confession is
> made unto salvation." (Rom 10:9-10)

It is not simply the words that proceed from the mouth but the heart condition that is the issue. Salvation happens when a person believes. The person that believes will not be disappointed.

> "For the scripture saith, Whosoever believeth
> on him shall not be ashamed." (Romans 10:11)

The word "ashamed" in the KJV means "brought to shame". It does not carry the idea of embarrassment. Romans 10:9-11 teach us that when a person comes to the point where he verbally professes from the heart belief in the risen Savior, he is saved and will not be disappointed. That same promise of security is made to both Jewish believers and Gentiles believers. Whoever calls, no matter what their race, will be saved.

> "For there is no difference between the Jew and
> the Greek: for the same Lord over all is rich unto
> all that call upon him. For whosoever shall
> call upon the name of the Lord shall be saved."
> (Romans 10:12-13)

Paul continues by saying that a person who calls on the name of the Lord is one who has already believed. Paul asks rhetorically

> "How then shall they call on him in whom they have not believed? ..." (Romans 10:14)

The idea is that calling on the name of the Lord is the result of someone who has already placed saving faith in the One being called upon. When Ananias admonished Paul to follow in believer's baptism and cleanse away his sins -- calling upon the name of the Lord -- he was admonishing Paul to savingly believe. Only by trusting Jesus Christ is someone cleansed, forgiven and justified. That is a heart matter.

> "With the **heart man believeth** unto righteousness..." (Romans 10:10).

Water baptism is a physical act that testifies to a spiritual reality -- salvation, but it does not enact or contribute to salvation. What Ananias was telling Paul was "All right, get up and get going for Jesus. Trust him. Get baptized. Call on his name. Get saved." Ananias was not giving a formula, pattern or prescription for witnessing when he says this to Saul. Neither was he giving a particular order for how salvation was achieved.

The fact that Ananias included a reference to baptism in his admonition to Saul of Tarsus does not indicate that water baptism is an essential ingredient to salvation. It does suggest that people who have truly trusted Christ will express that faith by following in believer's baptism. If they refuse to do that, it is good cause to suspect that they have never trusted the Savior for salvation to begin with.

Frank I. Snyder

Bibliography

Cymbala, Jim, *Fresh Wind, Fresh Fire,* Zondervan Publishing House Grand Rapids, MI 1997.

Gill, John, *John Gill's Exposition of the Entire Bible*

Green, J. B., McKnight, S., & Marshall, I. H., *Dictionary of Jesus and the Gospels,* InterVarsity Press: Downers Grove, Ill., 1992.

Hagin, Kenneth E,. *Seven Vital Steps To Receiving the Holy Spirit,* Faith Library Publications, Kenneth Hagin Ministries Inc., P.O. Box 50126 Tulsa OK 74150, 1980

Hawthorne, G. F., Martin, R. P., & Reid, D. G., *Dictionary of Paul and His Letters*, InterVarsity Press: Downers Grove, Ill. 1993.

Horton, Michael Scott, *Power Religion: The Selling Out of the Evangelical Church,* Chicago, Moody Press

Jensen, Jerry, *Baptists and the Baptism of the Holy Spirit,* Full Gospel Businessmen's Fellowship International 836 S. Figueroa St. Los Angeles 17, CA, 1963.

Johnson Arthur L., *Faith Misguided: Exposing the Dangers of Mysticism,* (Chicago: Moody Press, 1988)

Kaiser, W. C., *Hard Sayings of the Bible*, InterVarsity: Downers Grove, IL, 1997, c1996.

Lloyd-Jones, Martin, *The Sovereign Spirit; Discerning His Gifts,* Harold Shaw Publishers, Wheaton IL, 1985.

MacArthur, John, *The Charismatics: A Doctrinal Perspective,* Zondervan Publishing House, Grand Rapids, MI, 1978.

MacArthur, John, *Reckless Faith: When the Church Loses Its Will To Discern,* Crossway Books: Wheaton, IL, 1994.

White, John, *When The Spirit Comes With Power,* Intervarsity Press, Downers Grove, Illinois 60515 1988.

ABOUT THE AUTHOR

Pastor Frank Snyder has been in fulltime ministry for over 30 years. He is an ordained minister who received his Bachelor of Arts in Bible from Bob Jones University in Greenville, SC and his Master of Arts in Bible Exposition from Pensacola Christian College. He has also taken graduate level course work at several educational institutions.

Pastor Snyder's past ministry positions include youth pastor, minister of music, and associate pastor. He has served as a Senior Pastor since 1979, and is currently at Calvary Baptist Church of Quincy, Michigan.

In conjunction with his pastoral responsibilities, Pastor Snyder has served as a jail chaplain, a police chaplain, and the Board Chairman of Women & Teens Pregnancy Center in Pontiac, Michigan. He is currently the Chaplain for the Coldwater, Michigan Post of the Michigan State Police.

Pastor Snyder and his wife Cyndy are the parents of five children and presently have 12 grandchildren.

Made in the USA
Charleston, SC
29 September 2012